Acknowledgments

Come on up for the Rising ... The motivational power of **15 Strong** resonated not only with the Miami Heat, but with the championship collaborative efforts of the NBA and EventDay Media ... *Can't see nothin' in front of me* ... Similar to the Diesel, everything from the photos perspective flawlessly ran through Joe Amati whose championship presence, book experience and attention to detail in working through thousands of high-energy, portrait and access images throughout the two-week run was beyond terrific ... *Can't see nothin' coming up behind* ... Kevin Wright and Dave Bonilla supplied the frontcourt photos assistance ensuring that they had the Diesel's back in all double- and triple-coverage situations and came through every single time ... *I make my way through this darkness* ... John Fawaz — the Manhattan Beach legend — I couldn't ask for a more talented and professional writer as a running mate, who gives a huge shout out to his lovely wife, Joycelyn, on this unbelievably special project ... *I can't feel nothing but this chain that binds me* ... Andrew Pearson, the ultimate sixth man off the bench, provided a spark whenever called upon, which was early and often ... *Lost track of how far I've gone* ... Stacey Kerr assisting with the myriad of details and questions, which were plentiful ... *How far I've gone, how high I've climbed* ... At EventDay Media, Tom Pokorny, who similar to Riles, not only ensured that everyone maintained their focus through the dramatic shifts of the series but provided an enormous amount of support and then some ... *On my back's a 60-pound stone* ... Tammy Davis, similar to Dwyane Wade, came through in the clutch every single time, redefining peak performance on command, not only in keeping the team afloat but on championship course while flawlessly assisted behind the scenes by Lori Porter and Michele Rowe ... *On my shoulder a half-mile line* ... Michelle Fusillo and her supremely talented design team of George Burgess and Adam Gilardi over-delivering once again with next to nothing on the shot clock but somehow produced beautiful, skillfully designed pages ... *Come on up for the rising* ... The ultimate editorial safety net of Cynthia Dusenbery, Ron Koch, J.J. O'Malley and Shawn Akers was huge as always ... *Come on up, lay your hands in mine* ... Andy Bernstein, Nat Butler and Jesse D. Garrabrant — thank you ... *Come on up for the rising* ... Pat Riley, Randy Pfund, Dwyane Wade, Michael McCullough, Jeff Craney, Tim Donovan, Rob Wilson, Kim Stone, Michael Lissack and the entire Heat organization for their first-class assistance throughout the process ... *Come on up for the rising tonight* ... **15 Strong** wouldn't be complete without the extraordinary support of Steve Herbst — along with Charlie Rosenzweig, Michael Levine, Jeff Kaiser and Andrew Shaffer who punctuated the project with timely assistance — thank you .... *Come on up, lay your hands in mine* ... And for my special team of 5 Strong — Jennifer, Emma, Christopher and Leah — a heartfelt thank you ... Li, li, li, li, li, li, li, li

— John Hareas, July 2006

Special Thanks

At NBAE Photos: Joe Amati, Dave Bonilla, Brian Choi, Kevin Wright, John Kristofick, Pam Costello, Bennett Renda, Victor Nicholson.

At NBAE: Adam Silver, Danny Meiseles, Steve Herbst, Paul Hirschheimer, Charlie Rosenzweig, David Denenberg, Marc Hirschheimer, Michael Levine, Tony Stewart, Rob Sario.

At the NBA: David J. Stern, Russ Granik, Sal LaRocca, Greg Economou, Brian McIntyre, Terry Lyons, Tim Frank, Greg Lassen, Stacey Kerr.

At the Heat: Micky Arison, Pat Riley, Randy Pfund, Andy Elisburg, Tim Donovan, Michael McCullough, Kim Stone, Jeff Craney, Rob Wilson, Michael Lissack, Brian Babin and the entire Heat organization.

At EventDay Media: Tom Pokorny, Tammy Davis, Lori Porter, Michele Rowe, Michelle Fusillo, George Burgess, Adam Gilardi, Cindy Dusenbery, Ron Koch, J.J. O'Malley, Shawn Akers, Pat Dreyer, Rob Wolf, John Schreiner, Vince Warren.

Photo Credits

Nathaniel S. Butler: 10, 11, 12,13, 23, 30, 35, 56, 57 61, 67, 68, 70, 71, 73, 74, 75, 78, 79, 82, 83, 84, 85, 86, 87, 88, 89, 90, 92, 93 **Andrew D. Bernstein:** Cover, 6, 7, 9, 11, 15, 30, 32, 37, 38, 40, 41, 44, 45, 48, 60, 64, 67, 73, 82, 86, 94, 95, 100, 105, 106, 107, 109, 110, 111, 112 **Jesse D. Garrabrant:** Cover, 8, 23, 26, 27, 31, 34, 43, 48, 54, 55, 56, 57 58, 69 72, 78, 79, 82, 95, 96, 97, 104, 108, 111 **Scott Cunningham:** 11, 45 **Fernando Medina:** Cover, 13, 14, 43, 48 **Al Messerschmidt:** 12, 13 **Lou Capozzola:** 12 **Chris Covatta:** 13, 36 **Barry Gossage:** 11, 12, 13 **D. Lippit/Einstein:** 14, 15 **Jennifer Pottheiser:** 15, 98, 99 **Victor Baldizon:** Cover, 2, 3, 15, 16, 19, 21, 26, 33, 39, 42, 43, 44, 50, 54, 56, 58, 59, 62, 78, 79, 82, 101 **Tim Heitman:** 22 , 63 **NBA Photos:** 25 **Layne Murdoch:** 29, 60, 61, 63, 64, 69 73 **Andy Hayt:** 36 **David Liam Kyle:** 38 **Kent Smith:** 42 **Noah Graham:** 45, 91, 100 **Joe Murphy:** 1, 80, 81, 98 **Kevin Colber:** 17, 19, 20, 21 **Amy Glanzman:** 17 , 18, 19 **Issac Baldizon:** 17, 19, 20, 21, 46, 47, 51, 52, 53, 85 **Elsa:** 18 **Garrett Ellwood:** 24, 50, 61, 65, 66, 71, 73 **Rocky Widner:** 49 **David Sherman:** 60, 61 **Glenn James:** 60, 61, 67, 74, 107, 109, 110, 111 **Stephen Dunn:** 61 **Chris Graythen:** 76, 77 **Randy Belice:** 78, 79, 102, 103, 108 **Ronald Martinez:** 84, 94

2005-06 NBA CHAMPIONS DVD

Relive the excitement of The Finals with the Official 2005-06 NBA Champions DVD, featuring exclusive behind-the-scenes footage and interviews. From the season-opener to the Game 6 clincher, this special edition DVD highlights one of the greatest seasons in Miami Heat history. Available wherever videos are sold.

PUBLISHED BY:

EventDay Media. 1801 W. International Speedway Blvd., Daytona Beach, FL 32114

15 STRONG

15 STRONG

15 STRONG

15 STRONG

15 STRONG

CONTENTS

15 STRONG

It's More Than a Slogan, It's a Burning Desire

By Dwyane Wade

nfinished business. That was the prevailing feeling as we approached the 2005-06 season. When you come within 90 seconds of reaching the NBA Finals and don't do it, you're not going to have an enjoyable summer — I certainly didn't. The missed opportunity served as a driving force for us. We felt like we should have been representing the Eastern Conference and we weren't going to allow

another opportunity to slip through if we had the chance. Next thing you know, we're welcoming eight new players to training camp shortly after the team pulled off the biggest trade in NBA history, which involved 13 players and five teams. I remember guys thinking, "We had a great team the year before, so why the change, especially now?" I would be lying if I said that we didn't have doubts, not with the players coming in but about changing what we believed to be an already great team.

Early in the season, we were playing .500 ball, so those doubts only grew bigger, not only internally, but also from the media following the team. Our coach at the time, Stan Van Gundy, stepped down in early December, and things became even more uncertain. At the time, we were a confused team. We hadn't played that well, but we

had also been without Shaq for 18 games. Once Pat Riley came in as head coach, we didn't have time to look back. The only direction left to go was forward in order to get our season back on track.

When Coach Riley took over, I didn't know what to expect, but I had faith. When one of the greatest coaches in the history of the game becomes your coach, you know you are in good hands. It was an honor. One of the first things he told us was that we were going to turn into more of a power team, which was a departure from how we had played under Coach Van Gundy. After three games, however, I knew I was going to love our new style because I was getting more opportunities and fast breaks. Coach Riley helped me improve my overall game. If I played poorly or if I played well, he always pointed out something to show me the way

it was supposed to be done.

"If you want to be a winner," he said, "this is what you are going to have to do and what you should try to do."

Who am I to argue with him? So, I always tried to do it.

It took us awhile to adjust to the new style. Things didn't really click for us until, coincidentally, a 36-point loss to the Mavericks in Dallas on national television February 9. We were embarrassed and humiliated. In the team meeting after the loss, I remember Gary Payton standing up and asking what it was going to take to get better.

Coach Riley answered, "It's time to follow the leader."

We did. Any individual agendas — ranging from who shoots, who plays, what the rotation is — all took a back seat. The loss was a wake-up call, and we collectively decided to play as a unit beginning with our next game, three days later, versus the Pistons. We came from behind to win that game and immediately rolled to nine more victories. In those 10 consecutive wins, we came back eight times during the fourth quarter.

Even though we sort of sputtered toward the end of the regular season, losing six of our last 10 games, we knew we had the second seed in the Eastern Conference wrapped up.

Once the playoffs came around, there was a fair amount of people predicting that we would get knocked off, and that Chicago could be the team to do it, especially after they came back to tie the series. I think we really underestimated the Bulls, but we took their best punch. Outside of The Finals, that was probably the hardest series we played and one of the hardest that I've ever been a part of in my young career.

The next series against the New Jersey Nets started off poorly for us, as we lost Game 1 by 12 points. Once again, our downfall was predicted. But, we bounced back after realizing that our problems were coming from the defensive side of the ball — too many transition points and not enough rebounding. The key was to get back to playing as a team, which we did with the help of a huge performance from Antoine Walker in Game 2. From there, we rolled into Detroit, the series we had been waiting for all season long. We knew we could defeat this team if we played well. We had a lot of confidence in ourselves, and with Cleveland playing them so tough in the previous round, we saw the way they could be beaten. It took six games, but we got it done.

After the first two games of the NBA Finals, the doubters were out again with talk that the series wouldn't make it back to Dallas — a point that bothered us, but one that didn't surprise us since we had been underestimated all year. In fact, it lit a fire under us to go out and prove our point. Even during Game 3 when we were down 13 with 6:34 left, we still believed. We believed, becoming only the third team in NBA Finals history to win four straight against a great Dallas team.

In the end, it really was about "15 Strong" for us, a motto that came to represent togetherness and dedication to one another. No matter if we were high or low, through thick and thin, we always stuck together as a team. A lot of the guys on this team — Alonzo, Gary, Antoine — were doubted because they had never won a championship despite their individual success. It's just great when you can go out there and prove people wrong, and do it the right way. We all made plays to get to this point and achieve this goal, and that is what team basketball is all about ... 15 Strong.

A Star Is Born
Miami Heat Grows Into Its Name

n May 1986, former NBA player and coach Billy Cunningham and Broadway producer Zev Bufman announced plans to bring an NBA expansion team to Miami. They moved fast — before the end of the year, they had formed an ownership group, broken ground on a new arena, and picked a nickname. ❧ The NBA, duly impressed, granted the group an expansion franchise in April 1987.

The Miami Heat were born, though their entry into the league would be less than auspicious.

As the Heat gathered for their first practice in 1988, forward/center Scott Hastings, a career backup, looked around and said, "I'm worried. I might be the best player here."

Hastings had reason to be worried. The Heat were young — very young — and they struggled, even by expansion-team standards. Miami lost its first 17 games to set a record for most losses to begin a

season. The Heat finally won their first game on December 14, 1988, when they defeated the Clippers 89-88 in Los Angeles.

"I'm glad we won that one, because if we didn't, I don't know when we would have," said Ron Rothstein, the Heat's first coach and now an assistant with the team.

"Now, when people ask who we play for, we can tell them," Rony Seikaly said after the first win. The Heat threatened the record for worst record in a season

MIAMI HEAT

1986

1986: Billy Cunningham and theatrical producer Zev Bufman formally apply for an NBA expansion franchise.

1987

1987: The NBA officially announces its plans to expand the league by four teams. Miami will begin play during the 1988-89 season in the Eastern Conference's Midwest Division after paying a $32.5 million entry fee.

1988

1988: The Heat selects Rony Seikaly with the ninth selection of the 1988 NBA Draft.

1989

1988-1989: The first game in Miami Heat history ends unsuccessfully as they lose 101-80 to the Los Angeles Clippers in front of a sellout crowd of 15,008 on November 5, 1988. Rory Sparrow nets the first bucket in team history. Their first win would wait until December 14 when they defeat the Clippers 89-88.

With the fourth pick in the 1989 NBA Draft, the Heat selects Glen Rice, the Big Ten Conference's all-time leading scorer while at Michigan.

Rory Sparrow records the first triple-double (24 points, 10 rebounds, 10 assists) in Heat history on April 18, 1989, in the Heat's win over Dallas.

until they won nine games in the last two months to finish 15-67.

Things got better for Miami, thanks, in part, to Seikaly, the first player selected by the club in the NBA Draft. The 6' 11" center played six seasons in Miami, and he joined forward Glen Rice (drafted in 1989) and guard Steve Smith (drafted in 1991) to lead the Heat to their first playoff berth in 1992.

The Heat stumbled a bit the next season, then rebounded to post their first winning record (42-40) in 1993-94. But, the Heat lost again in the first round of the playoffs, which prompted an overhaul that resulted in the departure of Seikaly and Smith. In February 1995, the Arison family purchased controlling interest in the club, and Micky Arison took over as managing general partner.

One of Arison's first moves was to hire Pat Riley as president and head coach. Riley, who had led the "Showtime" Lakers to four NBA titles and guided the Knicks to the 1994 NBA Finals, had reached the playoffs in each of his 13 seasons as coach. He immediately set about building a winner in Miami.

First on his shopping list: A dominant big man, like Riley had in Los Angeles (Kareem Abdul-Jabbar) and in New York (Patrick Ewing). Riley acquired Alonzo Mourning from Charlotte, and they became an ideal duo of driven coach and driven player.

Led by the trio of Mourning, Tim Hardaway and Jamal Mashburn, the Heat won or shared the Atlantic Division title four consecutive seasons (1996-97 through 1999-00). Miami won a club-record 61 games in 1996-97, and the Heat became one of the NBA's glamour teams. They became a Miami hot spot, as the stars from South Beach ventured indoors for Heat games, especially after they moved into the new American Airlines Arena for the 1999-00 season.

But, Miami could not parlay its regular-season success into playoff glory. The Heat lost to Chicago in 1996 and 1997, then lost to their bitter rivals, the Knicks, in three consecutive years (1998, 1999 and 2000). Making matters worse, Miami was seeded second in 1998 and was the top seed in 1999.

Undeterred, the Heat prepared for another run at the title in 2000-01. But, before the season began, doctors diagnosed Mourning with a life-threatening kidney disease. He played

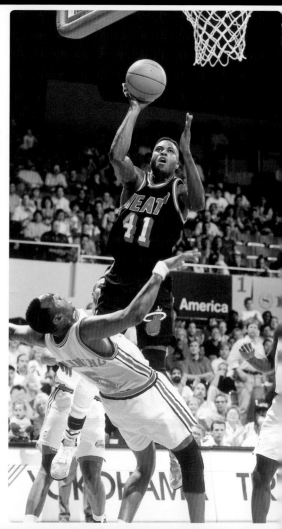

1990

1989-1990: The Heat move from the Midwest Division to the Atlantic Division.

Rony Seikaly is named the NBA's Most Improved Player, averaging 16.4 points per game and 10.4 rebounds.

1991

1990-1991: Kevin Loughery takes over as head coach for Ron Rothstein.

1992

1991-1992: Miami improves its record by 14 games and finishes at 38-44, good enough for the eighth playoff spot and the first in franchise history.

1992-1993: Harold Miner wins the 1993 Gatorade Slam Dunk Championship at NBA All-Star Weekend.

1993

1993-1994: The Heat wins their first playoff game, beating Atlanta 93-88 behind Steve Smith's 22 points.

1994

1994-1995: On February 13, 1995, the Arison family purchases all of Lewis Schaffel and Billy Cunningham's interest in the team. Micky Arison is named the club's Managing General Partner.

Glen Rice wins the NBA Long Distance Shootout at All-Star Weekend and Harold Minor takes his second slam dunk crown.

1995

1995-1996: Pat Riley is hired as the team's President and Head Coach on September 2, 1995.

The Heat acquires Alonzo Mourning, Pete Myers and LeRon Ellis on November 3 in a deal that sends Glen Rice, Matt Geiger and Khalid Reeves to Charlotte.

1996

Miami obtains Tim Hardaway prior to the trading deadline on February 22, 1996.

Alonzo Mourning becomes the first Heat player selected to the NBA All-Star Game.

1996-1997: Miami posts its best record, finishing the season at 61-21. In the playoffs they bounce back from a 3-1 deficit to defeat the Knicks in the Eastern Conference Semifinals before falling to Chicago.

1997

The Heat acquires Jamal Mashburn from Dallas on February 14, 1997, in exchange for Sasha Danilovic, Kurt Thomas and Martin Muursepp.

Ike Austin is named the NBA's Most Improved Player.

Pat Riley is named NBA Coach of the Year, becoming the first coach in NBA history to win the honor with three different franchises.

1997-1998: Pat Riley becomes the most successful coach in Heat history (134 wins) with Miami's 91-81 victory over Cleveland.

only 88 games in the next three seasons, and the Heat went from NBA title aspirants to the middle of the pack.

After missing the playoffs for the first time in his career (in 2001-02 and 2002-03), Riley stepped down as coach, handing the reins to longtime assistant Stan Van Gundy. When guard Anthony Carter accidentally failed to excercise his option, the Heat suddenly found themselves with cap room, allowing them to sign free agent Lamar Odom. The transition, however, was not smooth at first as Miami started 0-7 in 2003-04. But, behind Lamar Odom and a fabulous rookie named Dwyane Wade, Van Gundy turned things around. Miami finished 42-40, a 17-game improvement over the season before, and won a playoff series. The Heat were a team on the rise.

That rise became meteoric when Riley acquired Shaquille O'Neal in the summer 2004. The 7-foot-1-inch center, one of the greatest players in NBA history, already had three titles and showed up in Miami hungry for another ring. More important, though still dominant at age 32, O'Neal was willing to defer to Wade, the Heat's budding superstar.

In Shaq's first season, Miami improved by another 17 games, to 59-23, the best record in the East. Mourning, who had undergone a kidney transplant, returned to the team as O'Neal's backup. The Heat took a 3-2 lead over Detroit in the 2005 Eastern Conference Finals but, with Wade hobbled by a rib injury, they lost Games 6 and 7.

Riley transformed the roster during the summer, then took over as coach 21 games into the 2005-06 season after Van Gundy stepped down. Though their regular-season performance was disappointing, the Heat got healthy at the end of the season and coalesced in time for an impressive run in the 2006 NBA Playoffs.

"We've had a lot of near misses," Riley said after Miami defeated Detroit to advance to the 2006 NBA Finals. "We've had very good teams that I thought were championship contenders. We had a major, major setback with Zo's kidney ... and took two years to rebuild.

"But, ever since Shaquille O'Neal showed up on the scene, this team has been a legitimate contender, and we have put the pieces around him."

1998

1998-1999: Alonzo Mourning passes Rony Seikaly to become the Heat all-time leader in blocked shots (611) on April 1, 1999.

1999

Tim Hardaway passes Bimbo Coles to become the Heat all-time leader in assists (1,947) on April 22, 1999.

Alonzo Mourning is named NBA Defensive Player of the Year, averaging 3.91 blocks per game.

Heat assistant coach Bob McAdoo, a five-time NBA All-Star and two-time NBA champion, is elected to the Naismith Basketball Hall of Fame on May 24, 1999.

2000

1999-2000: Miami begins play in the American Airlines Arena on January 1, 2000.

Alonzo Mourning is elected the NBA Defensive Player of the Year for the second consecutive season — only the fifth player in NBA history to do so — and finishes third in the voting for NBA MVP.

The Heat and Knicks become the first two teams in history to play each other four consecutive seasons in the playoffs while having the series go the maximum number of games.

2001

2000-2001: Pat Riley earns his 1,000th career victory on Opening Night by beating the Orlando Magic, becoming only the second head coach in NBA history to achieve that milestone and the quickest head coach in any of the four major professional sports. Riley also leads the Heat to the playoffs for the 19th consecutive time in his coaching career, breaking the NBA record of 18 consecutive playoff appearances set by Red Auerbach (1949-1966).

Alonzo Mourning returns for the final 13 games of the season after being diagnosed with the kidney disorder focal glomerulosclerosis and posts averages of 13.6 points, 7.8 rebounds and 2.38 blocks.

2002

2001-2002: The Heat records the 500th victory in franchise history, topping Seattle 87-85 on November 6, 2001.

Alonzo Mourning is awarded the J. Walter Kennedy Citizenship Award.

2003

2002-2003: On March 11, 2003, Pat Riley becomes the only coach in NBA history to record 350 wins with two different franchises.

Caron Butler breaks the Heat rookie single-season scoring record (1,155) previously held by Sherman Douglas.

On October 24, 2003, Pat Riley steps down as head coach to concentrate more on being team president. He is succeeded by longtime assistant Stan Van Gundy, who becomes the first coach in Heat history to win his first playoff game in his first season.

2004

2003-2004: With the fifth pick in the 2003 NBA Draft, the Heat selects Dwyane Wade from Marquette University.

2004-2005: On July 14, 2004, the Heat acquires Shaquille O'Neal from the Lakers in exchange for Caron Butler, Lamar Odom, Brian Grant and a future first-round pick.

2005

2005-2006: The largest trade in NBA history sent Boston's Antoine Walker to Miami as part of a five-team, 13-player deal in August. The Heat also received point guard Jason Williams, forward James Posey, guard Andre Emmett and rights to Roberto Duenas of Spain.

Twenty-one games into the season, Stan Van Gundy resigned as head coach. Team President Pat Riley returned to the bench as coach. Van Gundy remained with the Heat to evaluate free agents and assist other projects.

The Heat defeated the Dallas Mavericks to win the team's first NBA championship on June 20, 2006. The Heat joined the 1969 Boston Celtics and 1977 Portland Trail Blazers as the only teams in NBA history to win the title after losing the first two games of The Finals.

Satisfaction
Guaranteed
Heat Bask in Glow of First
NBA Championship

The championship celebration began about 2 p.m. on a Friday, but, really, that was a mere formality. It actually began in earnest 72 hours earlier as fans flocked Ocean Drive and neighboring streets in the world famous South Beach area 1,300 miles from where their heroes had clinched the franchise's first NBA championship in dramatic fashion.

No one enjoyed the championship achievement more than the architect of the Heat's championship dreams — the man who unveiled the grandest of visions for the seven-year-old franchise on a cruise ship appropriately named Imagination. It was there, September 2, 1995, in the Dynasty Lounge when Pat Riley took the reins and dared to dream:

"I imagine in my mind the symbolic championship parade right down Biscayne Boulevard," Riley said.

Now, nearly 11 years later and a little more than a Dwyane Wade bounce pass away from where that prophetic statement came to life, Riley experienced the parade firsthand as the dream became reality. It was more beautiful than even he imagined. More than 250,000 Floridians converged on Biscayne Boulevard as thousands upon thousands of silver flakes shot out of confetti canyons, blanketing the brightest of blue Miami skies as flat-bed trucks and buses slowly made their way along the three-mile parade route as players waved and thanked their supporters.

Few outside the organization would have predicted the scene eight months

earlier. Doubts swirled amid a major roster upheaval, an early season coaching change and a myriad of questions about whether a team that was a minute and a half from reaching the NBA Finals a year ago had what it took to overthrow the reigning Eastern Conference Champion Detroit Pistons.

No one had more at stake or wanted this championship as badly as Riley, the man who went against conventional wisdom and trusted the instincts that had served him so well in the past. With four championships as head coach of the Lakers, not to mention the other two he earned as a player and assistant coach in Los Angeles, Riley knows all about championship blueprints. The seventh one, though, won 18 years after he last coached the Lakers to the NBA promised land, would be the sweetest one of all.

"I'd give up six of them for this one. I just would have," said Riley after the Game 6 clincher in Dallas. "I would have traded them all in for this one. It's not disrespectful to any of them that I won, but, after 18 years and chasing, you know, you keep chasing it, you keep chasing it and you get tired. So, this gives me a sense of absolute freedom."

Did victory bring vindication? Maybe in some people's minds, but Riley's place in NBA history as one of the greatest coaching minds was secure long ago, and with it, his eventual place in the Naismith Memorial Basketball Hall of Fame. It's the competitor in the 61-year-old Riley — the one who invested so much in the franchise, endured, along with his players, the heartbreaking playoff losses and near misses in the late 1990s to the New York Knicks, who needed this title to finally be able to exhale.

"This is the best. For so many reasons. It just is," Riley said. "When I was younger, it didn't have the same meaning. It came at the right time in my life."

The celebration intensified by a few notches at a rally outside AmericanAirlines Arena when the world's tallest emcee grabbed the microphone and took over.

"Can you dig it?!!!!!!!!!!!!" Shaquille O'Neal shouted to the thousands in attendance.

A veteran of three championship celebrations in Los

Go Gators!
Haslem, Williams Honed College Skills at Florida

As the vehicles carrying Heat players cruised slowly under a nearly cloudless sky along Biscayne Boulevard during Miami's championship parade, one had to wonder what was going through the minds of Udonis Haslem and Jason Williams.

As college players at the University of Florida, they helped build a growing basketball legacy before helping to bring the Larry O'Brien Trophy to South Florida for the first time.

Nearly 300 miles from Miami, Gainesville is known as a football factory, its legendary "Swamp" one of the craziest game-day celebrations around. But, things have changed a bit. Since Haslem became one of UF's more beloved four-year players after he joined the team the season following Williams' departure for the NBA in 1999, the school has gained as

much exposure for its hoops as for its pigskin prowess. The Gators won the NCAA's basketball national championship in 2006.

The inevitable match made in heaven took awhile to materialize — Williams made stopovers in Sacramento and Memphis before finally landing in the Heat backcourt, and Haslem took his hard-nosed approach to France for a season before signing with Miami in 2003-04.

In the end, however, two players who once donned the Gators' orange and blue couldn't help but smile as they basked in the white hot glare of the South Beach sunshine, their names etched in the NBA record books forever. — *Andrew Pearson*

Angeles, O'Neal is deft in leading such festivities, rapping and then later putting his coach on the spot.

"We all know Coach Riley's a great motivator. Who wants to see Coach Riley dance? Who wants to see Coach Riley dance? Give me some, Riley!"

Riles grooved to the encouragement of O'Neal.

"Go Coach!! Go Coach!! Go Coach!!" the big man shouted.

O'Neal, who guaranteed a Heat championship upon his arrival two years ago, earlier deviated from the parade route, exiting his vehicle to greet the fans as hundreds crossed barriers, hoping to get an up close glimpse of the legend.

"I want to make this one a little more personal," O'Neal said later. "I just wanted to get out to touch some people."

When Dwyane Wade wasn't clutching his Finals MVP trophy throughout the parade, he provided relief, cooling off the masses with some water gun fun, clearly basking in the championship moment.

"I'm just wowed about winning a championship," Wade said. "We deserve it. We put a lot of hard work in. Our fans deserve it."

It may have taken 18 years for the first title, but don't count on this being the last such gathering in Southern Florida. Not according to O'Neal.

"I've got four more years left. I think we can get two out of four. At worst."

Pat**Riley**
Coaching Legend's Return
Meant Misery for Foes

As the Miami Heat prepared to tip off this season, reporters asked team President Pat Riley why he dismantled a squad that had come so close to reaching the 2005 NBA Finals. "We were a minute and a half from The Finals — big deal," Riley said of Miami's loss to Detroit in Game 7 of the Eastern Conference Finals. "It's about winning a championship."

That's all it has ever been about for Riley, the man who once declared, "There is winning and there is misery." Forget the fact that the Heat went from last place to the brink of the NBA Finals in only two seasons. In Riley's world, unless you win the last game of the season, you are miserable.

So, roster changes were in order. No mere tweaking, but an overhaul. The core players remained. Shaquille O'Neal, Dwyane Wade, Alonzo Mourning and Udonis Haslem stayed.

True to form, Riley acquired mostly veterans, all of whom could handle the ball. Antoine Walker brought an inside-outside game, while Jason Williams offered quickness. Gary Payton intensified the defense, and James Posey added a three-point threat.

Many doubted whether the new pieces would fit. Riley, however, saw talented players who would give Miami added versatility and more firepower, reflecting the league-wide emphasis on offense. Moreover, the newcomers would complement the big two of O'Neal and Wade without disappearing in the fourth quarter.

"If we had brought back the exact same group we had last year, I think the results would be good, but we needed more talent," Riley told *The Washington Post* before the season. "We built the team around Shaquille that's a 'now' team. We want to get it done as quickly as we can. This is by far the best team I've been around since the ones I coached in Los Angeles."

Or, to quote another Riley maxim: "The thing about basketball players and basketball teams is they can't stay the same. You have to keep moving forward. You have to keep getting better."

The Heat, though, stumbled out of the gate. The team hardly had a chance to mesh when a big hole emerged in the middle. Two games into the 2005-06 season, O'Neal went down with a badly sprained ankle, an injury that sidelined him for 18 games.

By the time O'Neal returned, Riley was courtside, back as head coach after more than two seasons in the front office. He replaced Stan Van Gundy, who stepped down to spend more time with his family. Now Riley, who had built the team, would coach it as well.

"I have a responsibility to this team and to the players," Riley said about his decision to return to coaching. "I think,

"He's a **WINNER**, man. That's like a college professor that's been teaching for over 20 years and had people come out of his class with a bachelor's degree — summa cum laude."

— **Alonzo Mourning**

right now, at this moment, that I'm the best person to do that."

Indeed. As the team president, Riley assembled a group of talented but headstrong veterans who were asked to assume lesser roles. Melding them required someone equally as headstrong.

As the coach, Riley certainly had the credentials: the third-most victories (1,110) in NBA history and four championships. However, he is an old-school leader, an intense and demanding taskmaster. He challenged players mentally and physically. His preparation was unrivaled. His practices were the stuff of legend, often more grueling than the games.

"Pat is going to push and push and push," former Lakers' great Magic Johnson said hours after Riley's return. "If those guys aren't mentally tough, they're in for a rude awakening. ... It's a new day starting tomorrow in that practice. Trust me."

Would the players adapt? Or, would the Heat implode?

As it turned out, Riley was the one who adapted, as he had done throughout his coaching career. In Los Angeles (1981-

Pat Riley played with the 1972 title-winning Los Angeles Lakers.

Pat**Riley**
By the Numbers

Only the second coach in NBA history (Red Auerbach is the other) to lead a team to The Finals in three different decades, and the second head coach to lead three different teams (the Miami Heat, Los Angeles Lakers and New York Knicks) to The Finals (the first was Alex Hannum, who coached the St. Louis Hawks, San Francisco Warriors, and Philadelphia 76ers).

NBA Coach of the Year with three different teams — 1989-90 (Los Angeles Lakers), 1992-93 (New York Knicks), 1996-97 (Miami Heat).

NBA championships (1982, 1985, 1987, 1988 and 2006)

9 Conference Championships

Selected as one of the Top 10 Coaches in NBA History (1996).

17 Divisional Championships

Prior to this season, Pat Riley's last NBA title came in 1988 with the Lakers. The 18-year span between championships is the longest by a coach, eclipsing Alex Hannum (nine years), who led the St. Louis Hawks to the 1958 title and guided the Philadelphia 76ers to the 1967 title.

171 postseason victories (second all-time behind Phil Jackson); 278 postseason games coached (first all-time).

1,151-589 all-time career record (41-20 this season)
Third highest victory total in NBA history.

1990), Riley won two titles (1982 and 1985) with the "Showtime" Lakers, and two (1987 and 1988) with a different kind of team that relied more on defense and rebounding than fast breaks. In New York (1991-1995) and Miami (1995-2003), he embraced the three-pointer and turned loose an aggressive defense.

In each instance, Riley took what he had and made the most of it, demonstrating another one of his maxims: "The challenge of competition always involves finding new ways to win."

When Riley returned to the bench in December 2005, he prepared as relentlessly as ever, but shifted his focus. Practice no longer served to make players game tough. Instead of scrimmages, he put his players on stationary bicycles to improve their conditioning. They watched film, analyzing their opponents and themselves. When they did take the floor, they rarely went full speed, and Riley declared Wade off limits. Riley's message: Save it for the games. Save it for the playoffs.

On offense, the Heat ran when they could, but mostly they went back to basics: Pound the ball inside to O'Neal and then turn the game over to Wade in the fourth quarter. When O'Neal played in Los Angeles, the Lakers won three titles using the same formula, with Wade assuming the role once played by Kobe Bryant.

Defensively, the Heat finished in the middle of the pack, not what one would expect from a Riley-coached team. They were vulnerable on the perimeter, but the Heat controlled the paint and, in typical Riley fashion, dominated the boards.

Still, the Heat did not look like champions for most of the season. Miami, which had a record of 11-10 when Van Gundy stepped down, went 41-20 under Riley, although the Heat compiled that mark mostly against weaker competition. They were 1-9 against the league's top four teams (Dallas, Detroit, San Antonio and Phoenix), a record that did not bode well for their championship aspirations.

If the Heat never seemed to gel during the regular season, it was largely because they rarely had their top eight players in uniform at the same time. Critics called the season a disappointment, writing Miami's epitaph even before the playoffs began. Few gave the Heat a chance of getting past Detroit if the teams met again in the Eastern Conference Finals; many predicted they would struggle in the earlier rounds, to either Chicago or New Jersey.

For Riley, such talk amounted to very little. The Heat's regular-season record of 52-30, though not dominant, was good enough for the number-two seed in the Eastern Conference. Despite all the injuries and turmoil, Miami was poised for a title run. It's all about winning a championship.

"You'd love to have the team you've put on a piece of paper," Riley said during the season's final week. "You'd love to have them every game, but that's not been possible for us because of health. ... I just hope and pray that by the playoffs, we have everybody healthy and on the same page, so we can go with a full complement of players and see where this train takes us."

That train, as it turned out, took Riley right where he expected it to go.

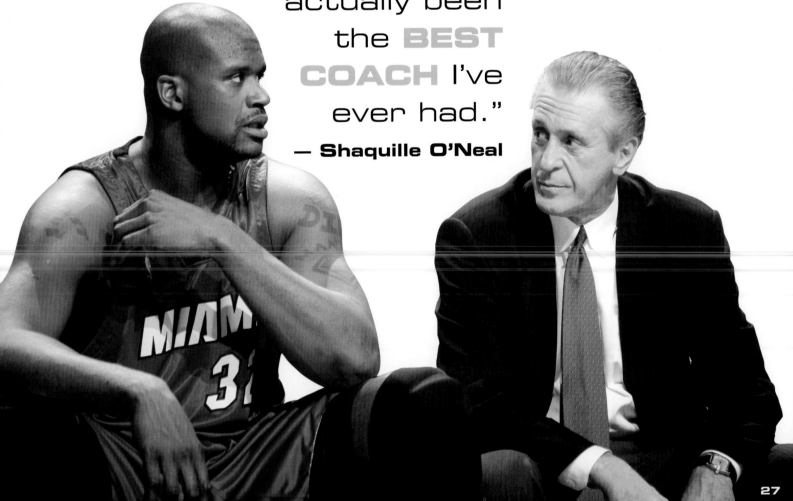

"I don't want to **HURT** anybody's **FEELINGS**, but he's actually been the **BEST COACH** I've ever had."

— Shaquille O'Neal

Shaquille O'Neal

Fourth NBA Ring Adds to Big Man's Legacy

When Pat Riley took over as Miami's coach in December, he told NBA superstar Shaquille O'Neal that he needed to lose weight. It was a tune O'Neal had heard from others. ❡ For Riley, though, the issue had greater urgency. Age and extra weight made O'Neal more susceptible to injury. He needed to pare the pounds so he would be more nimble and

durable. Shaq was plagued by foul trouble, as his lack of agility limited him to straight-ahead power moves on offense, while his career-long difficulties defending the pick-and-roll had worsened at the other end.

Shaq claimed his weight was 345; most estimates put it higher than 350. For the press, it became a game of "Guess Shaq's Weight," and everyone joining the contest received glassy stares from O'Neal, who has never reacted warmly to such questions. It was a familiar script: Coach says Shaq needs to lose weight, O'Neal says he needs the extra bulk to survive the pounding and that he will play his way into shape by the playoffs.

"Superman knows when to wake up," he said.

The wakeup call came earlier than expected, as Riley sat Shaq down in the fourth quarter of back-to-back games. O'Neal got the message.

"Pat called me out, said I didn't meet his requirements," O'Neal said later. "He said if I didn't meet them, I wouldn't be waived, but I'd be — what's it called? — deactivated."

Shaq ramped up his workouts on an exercise bike and changed his eating habits (five smaller, healthier meals per day, delivered to his home). When playoff time arrived, he carried 320 pounds, a weight

he had not seen since he played for the Orlando Magic early in his career.

Still, the whispers about O'Neal's supposed decline had become full-throated roars. He would never be a dominant center again. He missed 23 games during the season, including 18 in November and December because of a sprained ankle. He logged only 30.6 minutes and 20 points per game, both career-low averages. As the 2006 NBA Playoffs began, Shaq — and the Heat — were written off by many.

The first four games of Miami's first-round series seemed to confirm that diagnosis.

Though the series was tied 2-2, the young Chicago Bulls made the Heat look old and slow while winning two in a row. Shaq's performance in Game 3 had been the worst playoff outing of his career: eight points, four rebounds, five fouls and seven turnovers.

"I'm very, very humiliated," O'Neal said.

Number: 32
Height: 7'1"
Weight: 325
DOB: 3/6/72
College: LSU
Years in the League: 14

But, reports of Shaq's downfall — and that of the Heat — proved to be premature. O'Neal stopped fuming at the refs and adjusted his game, adding some new moves to avoid foul trouble. Miami won Game 5 and returned to Chicago for Game 6, which the Bulls were expected to win. Instead, O'Neal led an inspired defensive effort while dominating on offense, scoring 30 points on 13 of 24 shooting. He also had 20 rebounds as Miami coasted to the victory.

"My father called me this morning and said, 'Put your power game away, everybody's waiting for it,'" O'Neal said. "I've never really been an all-finesse player, but I gave it a shot, and it worked pretty well."

Shaq Draws
High Praise
from NBA Legend

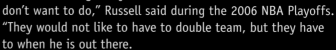

Shaquille O'Neal's numbers aren't as dominating as they once were, but he still has a greater impact on any game than any other player.

Who says? Bill Russell, and he should know. The Boston Celtics' legendary center won 11 NBA titles by doing things that never show up in a box score.

"He is using his presence to make [opposing teams] have to do things they don't want to do," Russell said during the 2006 NBA Playoffs. "They would not like to have to double team, but they have to when he is out there.

"Basic numbers are irrelevant. The only thing relevant is the final score — and he has an enormous amount to do with that."

Russell is also a big fan of Dwyane Wade, but he says O'Neal is still the Heat's most important player.

"Dwyane Wade ... is a great, great kid. In fact, I helped recruit him to go to college," Russell said. "But, Shaq may be more valuable to the team than Wade by virtue of his presence.

"Not only is Shaq playing really well, but his attitude is incredible. [It's really something] for him to say, 'Well, I'll take this role and do what I do for this team, and I'll do everything I can to make it easy for other guys.'"

Doubts were renewed four days later, however, when New Jersey ran Miami off the floor in Game 1 of their Eastern Conference semifinal. Foul trouble again limited Shaq's playing time and effectiveness — and, again, O'Neal adjusted.

The Heat won the next three games by turning up their defense, then closed out the series with a 106-105 victory at home. O'Neal posted solid, if unspectacular numbers, reflecting his reduced burden as the Heat relied more on Dwyane Wade and an improved group of role players.

"It's a lot easier for him if he isn't the focus," Riley said. "Going to him all the time, I don't know if he can carry it, but he can definitely finish a lot of things for us."

Finish he did. In the Eastern Conference Finals against Detroit, O'Neal shot 65.5 percent from the floor while averaging 21.7 points and 10.5 rebounds per game. The new, agile O'Neal defended the pick-and-roll better than ever, and he dominated the paint, forcing the Pistons to settle for jump shots. It was vintage Shaq and more.

O'Neal showed he could still carry the team in Game 6, when the flu slowed Wade. He tallied 28 points (on 12 of 14 shooting) and 16 rebounds to put Miami in the NBA Finals. Shaq continued to climb the ladder of big men, joining Wilt Chamberlain as the only center to lead three different teams to the NBA Finals while winning his fourth NBA title. For Shaq, who calls himself LCL (Last Center Left), the 2006 NBA Finals ultimately were about legacies — his and the one he had inherited.

"I would have thought there would be young guys coming in after me like I came in after all the other guys," O'Neal said about today's NBA, where 7-footers play facing the basket and shoot threes. "But, they don't come anymore. They just stand out and they shoot jumpers. I guess that's where the game is going for big guys.

"So, yeah, I'm the last of the Chamberlains and Bill Russells."

DwyaneWade
Flash Turns Heat Into a Champion

Dwyane Wade made the journey from little-known draft pick to superstar in, well, a flash. ✐ "It seemed like it happened overnight," Wade said in February 2005, midway through his second season in the NBA. ✐ The spotlight never shined on Wade (or a lot of other players) during the 2003 NBA Draft, also known as the LeBron James draft.

Not that he complained — the unassuming guard from Marquette University always has been more comfortable on the wing.

Besides, Wade had the attention he wanted (from NBA scouts), and his hometown Chicago Bulls stood ready to take him with the seventh pick. But, Miami, in need of a center, passed on several big men and selected him with the fifth pick. Pat Riley had seen the future, and it was Wade.

"How we plan on playing in the future is bigger and longer," Riley said. "Here is a guy that's 6-4. He's got a [long] wingspan. He's real long and athletic. ... He's an absolutely complete player who can get better."

Riley had visions of a versatile lineup that would run the floor and attack the basket, one that many — remembering his

days with Magic Johnson in Los Angeles — might call "Showtime East," featuring Wade as its centerpiece.

"I think Dwyane is going to surprise a lot of people," Riley said before Wade's rookie season. "He has the demeanor of a Joe Dumars. He's got the ability of a Gary Payton. I think he has the potential to have a huge, huge upside."

Three years later, we know that Riley committed that rarest of coaching feats — an understatement. Riley compared Wade to great players; now, at age 24, he is being compared to the all-time greats.

Though Wade made it look easy, it was not. His first three seasons included constant turnover among teammates and coaches, offensive changes and the intense glare of the national media. Lesser players have wilted under less, but, thanks to his

maturity and adaptability, Wade not only survived, he thrived.

Consider the circumstances:

2003-04: Riley steps down as coach before the season, replaced by Stan Van Gundy. Wade, Eddie Jones and Lamar Odom lead an up-tempo, fast-break offense. Miami finishes 42-40, a 17-game improvement over the previous season, and advances to the Eastern Conference Semifinals.

2004-05: Shaquille O'Neal arrives and nicknames Wade "Flash." The Heat slow things down and switch to a half-court offense. The NBA's newest version of the dynamic duo transforms Miami into an elite team. Wade becomes a household name, but the season ends with a disappointing near miss against the Pistons in the Eastern Conference Finals.

2005-06: A roster makeover brings in new faces, making the Heat into a hybrid — a half-court team that will try to run the floor when possible. Miami struggles early without the injured O'Neal. Van Gundy steps down and Riley returns as coach. The Heat somewhat right themselves, but cohesion

proves elusive. Few give the team a chance to overcome the Pistons in the East. Miami proves the doubters wrong, beating Detroit in the Eastern Conference Final and then defeating the Dallas Mavericks to claim the team's first NBA title.

Wade remained the one constant for Miami during the past three seasons. He got better and better amidst the whirlwind. He used his speed, quickness,

defensive teams. In Game 3, with Miami clinging to a 74-73 lead, he denied Detroit's Antonio McDyess on a dunk attempt at one end, then made a three-point play at the offensive end. Miami went on to win 98-83 to take a 2-1 series lead. The play was a microcosm of the series: The Pistons had no answer for Flash.

"He's the most dynamic player in the game right now," Detroit coach Flip

response for every strategy, and it was Detroit that reeled from his new moves and superb passes in traffic.

"I'll try anything, and if it works in practice, I'll do it in a game," Wade said.

That attitude reflects his relentless quest to improve, to be the best player in the game. The talent, the unyielding drive, the ability to play above the rim and make his teammates better — all that has earned

"He's the most DYNAMIC PLAYER in the game right now."

— Flip Saunders
Detroit Pistons Head Coach

and 39-inch vertical leap to attack the rim at every opportunity, undeterred by even the most intimidating big men. No matter how hard the foul, Wade sprung to his feet.

Wade complemented his aerial assault by improving his passing, outside shooting, ball handling and defense. That, in turn, opened up the lane for more drives and dunks. He averaged a career-best 27.2 points per game in 2005-06 while shooting 48.1 percent from the field.

In the 2006 Eastern Conference Finals, Wade shot 61.7 percent from the field against the Pistons, one of the league's top

Saunders said. "He can make something basically out of nothing."

The Pistons tried to keep Wade off balance with constant change — the long arms of Tayshaun Prince, the quickness of Lindsey Hunter and the physical play of Richard Hamilton, plus double teams, traps, and even some zone. Wade, though, had a

Wade some lofty comparisons.

Thanks, he says, but right now, he is having too much fun to think about it.

"I'm just a kid who loves to play the game of basketball," Wade said after hearing his name mentioned alongside Michael Jordan and Magic Johnson.

"Those guys — I'm not even close to that. I've got to win a lot of championships to get there."

Alonzo**Mourning**

Wait for Title Has Been Zo Long, Zo Good

The Miami Heat acquired Alonzo Mourning with the expectation of winning a championship. Neither expected it would take this long. ✦ *"I think about 13 years, and that's literally a lot of blood, a lot of sweat, a lot of ups and downs, so many disappointments year after year, it makes you appreciate this moment even more," Mourning said after Miami defeated*

Detroit in Game 6 of the 2006 Eastern Conference Finals. "This is a road less traveled. ... You have to treat it like it's your last step."

Life can change in an instant, as Mourning knows all too well. One moment he is one of the NBA's top centers, a 30-year-old superstar in his prime. He is celebrating his gold-medal victory playing for Team USA in the 2000 Olympics. He is about to tip off his ninth season in the league, leading a Heat team that is favored to win the Eastern Conference. The NBA title that has eluded him might finally be within reach.

The next moment doctors are telling him he has a serious kidney ailment. The condition is potentially life threatening. He will be sidelined indefinitely, maybe forever. For the man they call "Zo," nothing has been the same since.

Mourning played only 88 games in the next three seasons, missing the entire 2002-03 campaign. He then signed with the New Jersey Nets, but lasted only 12 games in 2003-04 before announcing his retirement. His condition had worsened, and he needed a kidney transplant.

In December 2003, Mourning received a kidney from his cousin in what he described as a life-saving operation. Doctors said that, if all went well, Zo could lead a normal life.

Basketball? Out of the question — or so it seemed.

Mourning could not stay away. He began working out as soon as the doctors would allow. Less than a year after the surgery, he returned to the court. By any measure, it was a remarkable comeback.

His excitement soon turned to frustration, however. The Nets were struggling as they tried to build a winner, and Mourning did not have the luxury of time. He had re-opened his window of opportunity, but it would soon close permanently. So, after a trade to Toronto and a buyout of his contract, Zo went to the place that afforded him the best opportunity for a title — Miami.

Questions abounded: Could Mourning, still a favorite of Heat fans, handle a reduced role as a reserve? How much did his medication affect his endurance? Could he co-exist with Shaquille O'Neal, a bitter rival for most of his career?

As for playing time, Mourning put those concerns to rest immediately.

Number: 33
Height: 6'10"
Weight: 261
DOB: 2/8/70
College: Georgetown
Years in the League: 14
(Missed 2002-03 season due to injury.)

"I've got pride," he said. "I want to play the game, but I understand the bigger picture. ... It's about accomplishing something I want to accomplish: winning a championship."

As it turned out, Mourning has played quite a bit. He averaged nearly 13 minutes per game with Miami last season, and even started two games in the postseason. He averaged 20 minutes per game in 2005-06, starting 20 games in place of an injured O'Neal. Zo made the most of his minutes, blocking 2.66 shots per game to rank third in the NBA.

"His role is that he's a leader," Heat coach Pat Riley said. "He's backing up Shaq, sparing him minutes. ... He's capable of making plays for us, but he's been a leader, a great leader for us and a great backup center."

Any tension with Shaq quickly evaporated. The two hit it off, with Shaq saying he and Zo had become "best friends." O'Neal has been appreciative of

his reduced burden and Mourning is grateful for the opportunity.

"He and I both want the same thing," O'Neal said. "We want to get it done."

The same could be said for Mourning and Riley. The two have long shared a single-minded obsession with winning an NBA title, to the exclusion of all else. When Zo joined the Heat in 1995, he endured one of Riley's grueling all-day practices — then worked out on his own for another two and a half hours. That's a Riley player if ever there was one. Riley built a team around Mourning that he thought would contend for the

NBA title. Instead, playoff heartbreak became an annual event. In 1996 and 1997, the Heat were thwarted by Michael Jordan and the Bulls, followed by three consecutive defeats (1998, 1999, and 2000) at the hands of the New York Knicks.

With all that history, plus another crushing postseason disappointment in 2005, and his own health to consider, no wonder Mourning brought a great sense of urgency to this year's playoffs.

"As soon as you step on the floor, a clock starts ticking, and none of us knows when it is going to stop," Mourning said during the 2006 Eastern Conference Finals. "You have to approach situations like this as, 'Man, this could be my last opportunity ... to play for something special.'"

Name Recognition

Role Players Know How to Bring the Heat

Wade. Shaq. Zo. *Those are the names everybody knows. But, the Heat's role players were hardly no-names.* ◀ *After Miami fell short in the 2005 NBA Playoffs, Pat Riley remade the team, keeping the core but surrounding it with a* new supporting cast. Most were veterans who had been stars elsewhere but now would be asked to play supporting roles.

Critics predicted disaster. Who would play defense? Would there be enough shots to go around? Could this group ever mesh?

Exhibit A was Antoine Walker, a talented, versatile forward who liked to launch three-pointers — a lot of them. During his first nine seasons in the NBA, Walker had always been the first or second option. How would he adjust to being option three or four?

"I had to accept being a role player and realizing 75 percent of our offense is through Shaq and Dwyane," Walker said. "I'm used to getting 17 or 18 shots a night. Here, you may get five a night, you may get 10, or you may get 18 shots. You just have to play your role when called."

Walker performed his part as cast, supplying three-point shooting and rebounding, and playing some defense. He ranked fourth on the team in scoring (12.2 points per game), posted his highest three-point field goal percentage (.358) since 2000-01, and was the only member of the Heat to play all 82 games.

Walker became a regular by season's end, and started every game during the postseason. He raised his scoring average in the playoffs, heeding Riley's desire that he take the ball to the hoop.

"He's a great guy," Riley said during the 2006 NBA Finals. "He's been a hard worker all year."

Doubts also surrounded Jason Williams, the talented and flashy (too flashy, according to most) guard that Riley acquired from Memphis. The mercurial Williams could break down any defense with his crossover dribble, bring wows with his passing, and elicit cheers with his treys. But, he also brought headaches with his turnovers.

PAYTON

D.ANDERSON

S.ANDERSON

Could he get the ball to Shaq in the post and Wade on the wing?

Yes, as it turned out. Williams so took to the role of point guard that Riley had to tell him to shoot more. He ranked 12th in the NBA in assists per turnover (2.87) and ranked third on the team in scoring (12.3 points per game), despite being hobbled by knee problems much of the season. When the flu slowed Wade in Game 6 of the Eastern Conference Finals, Williams stepped up. He scored 21 points (he made his first 10 shots), which helped the Heat run away for a 95-78 victory.

"We just came together as a group," Williams said. "Everybody thinks we all have egos and I think it's true — we all have egos, to a certain extent. I don't think our egos are as big as everybody thinks they are. We just came together and did what we have to do."

Williams, who played at the University of Florida, seemed very much at home in Miami, and the Heat benefited from his newfound maturity.

"Even if I may not look like I'm having that much fun, I am, because we are winning," Williams said. "If I get 20 points, good, if I don't, it's good. Winning cures everything for me."

Riley brought in Gary Payton for his defense, and he delivered on that end. At age 37, he played nearly 30 minutes per game in 2005-06, proving especially vital in the fourth quarter. But, it's Payton's offensive exploits — his game-winning shot in Game 3 of the NBA Finals, followed by a huge lay-up in overtime of Game 5 — that will always be remembered in Miami. Only fitting, perhaps, for no Heat player has coveted an NBA title as long as Payton.

The championship was also sweet for Udonis Haslem, a Miami native who grew up rooting for the Heat. Haslem is Riley's type of player: selfless, willing to do anything for the team, and a

KAPONO

POSEY

HASLEM

skilled, physical defender. One of only seven holdovers from the previous season, Haslem accepted a reduced role on offense without complaint. One thing he would not accept was lack of effort.

"Udonis speaks his mind," Riley said. "He's a no-nonsense guy. If he sees guys taking a step back or not pulling their part of the rope, he will let them know."

Haslem pulled more than his part during the 2006 NBA Finals, when he had the unenviable task of guarding Dallas' Dirk Nowitzki. The Heat forward did not back down, getting up on the Mavericks' forward and sticking to him. Even Nowitzki said that much of his poor performance in the series could be attributed to Haslem and the Heat defense.

Another defender who gave the Mavericks trouble was swingman James Posey, who regularly sacrificed his body to take a charge. He started at small forward for most of the regular season, and his three-point shooting (.403) thwarted many teams' attempts to double team Shaq or Wade.

Though Riley settled into a regular rotation of eight players by the playoffs, for much of the 2005-06 season the Heat

struggled with injuries. Players who stepped in during that time included veteran swingman Derek Anderson, who came from Houston in a February trade; forward Jason Kapono; defensive specialist Shandon Anderson; and center Michael Doleac.

Other contributors throughout the season rounding out the team's 15 Strong theme included Wayne Simien, Dorell Wright and Earl Barron.

In the end, according to Riley, the Heat's role players assumed a new role, that of a team. Just as he hoped.

"They're not a supporting cast. I don't look at it that way," Riley said. "They're all pros. They've been around. They know what to do.

"I know we're humbled by the opportunity because I don't think a lot of people believed we'd be here [in the NBA Finals], and, probably, there were some doubts on this team at one time. So, these guys are savoring the opportunity."

S E A

Parts of the Equation

Heat Players Pull Together for Title Season Drive

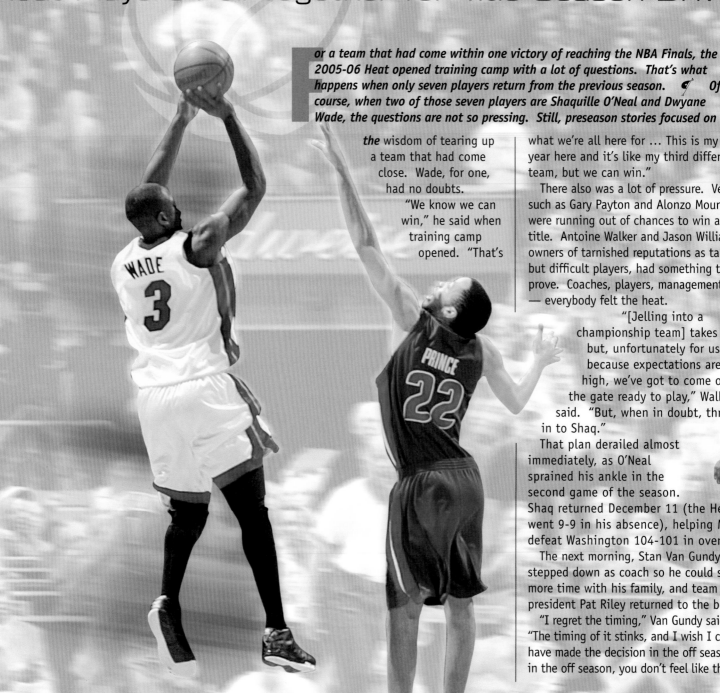

For a team that had come within one victory of reaching the NBA Finals, the 2005-06 Heat opened training camp with a lot of questions. That's what happens when only seven players return from the previous season. ✑ Of course, when two of those seven players are Shaquille O'Neal and Dwyane Wade, the questions are not so pressing. Still, preseason stories focused on

the wisdom of tearing up a team that had come close. Wade, for one, had no doubts.

"We know we can win," he said when training camp opened. "That's what we're all here for ... This is my third year here and it's like my third different team, but we can win."

There also was a lot of pressure. Veterans such as Gary Payton and Alonzo Mourning, were running out of chances to win an NBA title. Antoine Walker and Jason Williams, owners of tarnished reputations as talented but difficult players, had something to prove. Coaches, players, management — everybody felt the heat.

"[Jelling into a championship team] takes time, but, unfortunately for us because expectations are so high, we've got to come out of the gate ready to play," Walker said. "But, when in doubt, throw it in to Shaq."

That plan derailed almost immediately, as O'Neal sprained his ankle in the second game of the season. Shaq returned December 11 (the Heat went 9-9 in his absence), helping Miami defeat Washington 104-101 in overtime.

The next morning, Stan Van Gundy stepped down as coach so he could spend more time with his family, and team president Pat Riley returned to the bench.

"I regret the timing," Van Gundy said. "The timing of it stinks, and I wish I could have made the decision in the off season, but in the off season, you don't feel like this.

"I talked to Pat [about resigning] for the first time after the second game of the year, and Pat basically spent the last six weeks trying to convince me to think about it more and more ... to make sure that's really what I wanted to do."

The Heat, 11-10 when Riley took over, improved with O'Neal back in the lineup. But, they hardly had the look of a champion, padding their record (24-17 at the midway point) against weaker opponents while losing (badly) to the NBA's elite teams. Riley called the first half of the season "a 41-game disappointment."

The parts definitely were not fitting at that point. Injuries had hampered Williams, while Walker struggled to adjust to his new role coming off the bench and playing without the ball. O'Neal, carrying extra weight and starting to show his age (he turned 34 in March), was struggling. Wade proved to be the only constant. Riley, though, remained unconcerned.

"I have complete faith," he said. "That's how I operate. That's how I coach. I truly believe that, when all the parts are healthy ... this team can do something special."

Riley continued to preach that view and, eventually, his team proved him right. The turning point came February 9,

"It was a matter of time before guys bought into the system. A lot of teams jumped out of the gate and now look at them. It's a marathon."

— Antoine Walker

when Miami lost to Dallas 112-76 to fall to 30-20. In the locker room after the game, Payton spoke to the team, as did Udonis Haslem, one of the six holdovers from the previous season.

"That was one of the few times I felt like it was time to be vocal," said Haslem. "I just felt like it was a situation where we weren't playing as well as the talent on this team .... We weren't trusting each other. We weren't playing for each other. We weren't laying out on the floor for each other."

Three days later, Miami rallied from an 84-71, fourth-quarter deficit to defeat Detroit 100-98. Wade scored the Heat's final 17 points to give them their first victory (in eight tries) against one of the NBA's top four teams (Dallas, Detroit, Phoenix and San Antonio). Following the Detroit game, Miami went on to win 14 of their next 15 games. Although all but two of the victories came against teams with losing records, the stretch boosted the Heat's confidence as the playoffs approached.

"It was a matter of time before guys bought into the system," Walker said. "A lot of teams jumped out of the gate and now look at them. It's a marathon."

Just as the Heat seemed to be putting things together, injuries sidelined Williams, James Posey and Alonzo Mourning. Miami stumbled, losing nine of its last 17 games. The playoffs loomed, yet Riley described his team as "still a work in progress" while O'Neal said they were merely "bored."

Despite the lackluster ending to the regular season, the Heat expressed confidence. Their top eight players, who had excelled as a group when healthy, would be back for the postseason. Their 52-30 record had been good enough for the number-two seed in the Eastern Conference. Regardless of what went on in the regular season, they had an excellent shot at an NBA title, something that had eluded Shaq and Wade the year before and had eluded Payton and Mourning for more than a decade. They could not ask for anything more.

"Zo is playing for the minimum, Gary Payton is playing for the minimum, Antoine Walker took less than what he could get," Riley said during the 2006 NBA Playoffs. "There's a long list of players that have sacrificed not only financially but minutes, position, their egos, the kind of games they've had before ....

"While everybody else has been sort of taking them apart, they have been quietly becoming a team."

POSTSEASON

Unlikely Scenario

Gutsy Heat Bury Playoff Doubters

The Miami Heat, the team "built for the playoffs," began postseason play by splitting the first four games against the seventh-seeded Chicago Bulls. Though not unusual, even in a battle of a second seed against a seventh seed, it provided more fodder for the Heat's doubters. ⚡ Miami had reason to be concerned. During the two losses in Chicago, the Bulls had exploited the Heat's defense on

the perimeter and in transition, weak spots all season. Shaquille O'Neal had been in foul trouble. As they headed home for Game 5, the epitaph for the 2005-06 Heat was again being written, and not for the last time.

They found salvation from the usual place. Miami trailed by five points midway through the third quarter of Game 5, and the outlook was not promising. O'Neal was heading to the bench with his fourth foul, while Dwyane Wade had not been seen since injuring his hip in the first half.

But, as O'Neal checked out, Wade suddenly returned and immediately sparked a 16-6 run. The Heat, rejuvenated, clamped down on defense and won 92-78. Wade finished with 28 points, after O'Neal (16 points, 10 rebounds), Antoine Walker (17 and 7) and

James Posey (12 and 8) had helped keep the Heat in the game.

"Tonight we felt a little bit of pressure once Dwyane went down. It was a shock," said Heat coach Pat Riley. "We all got stunned, but we were able to weather the storm not knowing what was going to happen to him. Strange things happen when you think things are at their worst."

The uplift carried over to Game 6, as the Heat raced to an early lead and never were threatened. Miami's defense overwhelmed the Bulls, Shaq (30 points, 20 rebounds) dominated, and the role players shined in the Heat's 113-96 victory.

"There was a lot of pressure on us this series," Riley said. "From what I hear, not many people wanted us to win."

Turn up the Heat
Early Loss to Nets Not Fatal for Heat

Reports of the Heat's demise, greatly exaggerated throughout the 2005-06 season, reached the level of absurdity in the Eastern Conference Semifinals, when they were pronounced done after one game. Finished. Kaput. Gone fishing. ❧ Admittedly, it was a horrendous game, as New Jersey outscored Miami 38-21 in the first quarter and cruised to a 100-88 victory.

Yes, the Heat looked old and very ordinary. But, it was still only one game.

Pat Riley had built this team exactly for this situation. Yes, some of them were old by NBA standards, but that meant they would not panic. Instead, they would respond to adversity, and respond they did. In Game 2, Miami ran out to a 41-19 lead and never let up, winning 111-89.

"Our work begins now," Riley said after Game 2. "Maybe the other night was an aberration and tonight was an aberration. Now, we get down to reality and crunch it out."

The reality was that the Nets simply had no answer for Dwyane Wade and the growing contributions of the Heat's role players. New Jersey led 81-80 with 4:36 to play in Game 3, then watched helplessly as Wade (30 points, 10 assists, 7 rebounds) took over. He scored seven points in a 13-2 run that spurred Miami to a 103-92 victory.

Game 4 followed a similar script, only this time Wade (31 points) had help from Antoine Walker and Udonis Haslem, who each scored 20 points. Walker's three-pointers pushed the Heat to a double-digit lead in the third quarter, and after the Nets closed to one, Haslem had several key baskets and a huge rebound in the fourth. Miami won 102-92.

Leading 3-1, Miami returned home expecting a battle, and New Jersey did not disappoint. Miami, which had six players score in double figures, won 106-105, and Wade again figured prominently. He made six of 10 shots in the second half and his steal in the final seconds ended the Nets' last hope.

The Heat, left for dead after Game 1, suddenly looked like the team Riley had envisioned. Better late than never.

"Everybody knows we've got two of the best players in the league, but we've got to have everybody else fulfilling roles," Walker said. "We'd love for it to have happened earlier, but it's happening now, at just the right time."

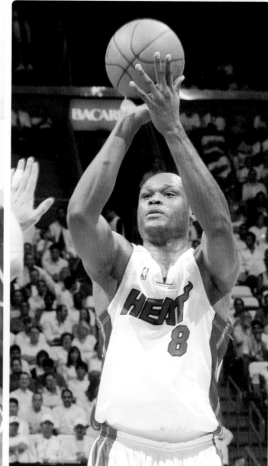

EASTERN CONFERENCE SEMIFINALS

Game 1 — New Jersey 100, Miami 88

Game 2 — Miami 111, New Jersey 89

Game 3 — Miami 103, New Jersey 92

Game 4 — Miami 102, New Jersey 92

Game 5 — Miami 106, New Jersey 105

Heat's Quest
Road to Eastern Conference Finals Goes Through Detroit

Detroit and Miami followed far different paths to their rematch in the 2006 Eastern Conference Finals. ❡ The Pistons, free of the turmoil that had plagued them the previous season, notched the NBA's best record (64-18) in 2005-06. They were a team with a capital T — a confident, selfless group that was hungry to reclaim the NBA title. Detroit was all but pre-ordained as the

Eastern Conference champion heading into the playoffs.

The 2005-06 Heat, on the other hand, had more than their share of turmoil and doubts, in contrast to the relatively placid season they enjoyed the year before. They had to deal with a coaching change, numerous injuries, and parts that did not seem to mesh. They seemed pre-ordained as the most likely upset victim heading into the playoffs.

By the time the teams met, however, roles were reversed. Detroit was coming off a seven-game series against Cleveland that had ground up their aura of invincibility. The Cavaliers had exposed Detroit's lack of offense and depth, and the Pistons' defense, though still one of the best, simply wasn't good enough to carry them.

The Heat, fresh off a five-game series against New Jersey, suddenly looked quite formidable. Unlike 2005, Shaquille O'Neal and Dwyane Wade were healthy, and also unlike

the previous year, they had a stronger supporting cast.

"We always had an excuse about last year ... and there's none now," Heat coach Pat Riley said. "We're rested, we're healthy, I think we're happy, and I hope we are humble."

By series end, the role reversal was complete, as the Heat came together and the Pistons came apart amidst accusations and excuses. Miami served notice by winning Game 1 in Detroit, taking an early lead and hanging on for a 91-86 victory despite Wade's foul trouble. In Game 2, Detroit had to hang on, as Wade (32 points) led a Miami rally that fell short, 92-88.

Even though the series was tied 1-1, the Heat clearly had the momentum heading back to Miami, and they did not let up. In Game 3, Miami built a double-digit lead, only to watch Detroit mount an 11-0 run to pull close at 74-73. After a timeout, Wade (35 points) answered with a three-point play, Shaq (27 points) made a hook, and Miami went on to win 98-83.

Miami struggled offensively in Game 4, but the Heat's defense bottled up the Pistons for an 89-78 victory. Wade, who did not score a field goal in the third quarter, poured in 12 fourth-quarter points to help Miami pull away. He finished with 31 points.

The Pistons, down 3-1, expressed confidence, citing

their recent record in elimination games. Detroit improved that mark with a 91-78 victory in Game 5, then the teams returned to Miami, where the Pistons' chances seemed to improve when Wade came down with the flu.

But, O'Neal and the Heat's understudies embraced the challenge in Game 6. Shaq owned the paint from the opening tip, finishing with 28 points (on 12 of 14 shooting) and 16 rebounds. Jason Williams (21 points) made his first 10 shots, and the Heat overcame Wade's illness (he had only 14 points) by shooting 55.7 percent from the field in a 95-78 victory.

"To be at the point where we are now on our way to the Finals is truly amazing for this organization," Wade said. "We went out there and played team basketball at the right time of year."

EASTERN CONFERENCE FINALS

Game 1 — Miami 91, Detroit 86	
Game 2 — Detroit 92, Miami 88	
Game 3 — Miami 98, Detroit 83	
Game 4 — Miami 89, Detroit 78	
Game 5 — Detroit 91, Miami 78	
Game 6 — Miami 95, Detroit 78	

The Finals

The Finals 1

Mavericks Take Game 1
The 'Jet' Swoops In, Steals Show

It's difficult to imagine that many in Texas considered spring football the state's second most popular sport. That notion never seemed more farfetched than on the eve of the 60th NBA Finals. ✐ Mavs Mania was rampant, engulfing Dallas like never before, evident at every turn as "Go Mavs!" signs were strewn throughout shops and buildings as fans proudly

wore their favorite Mav T-shirts, jerseys and hats — many wore all three. Showing that devotion for one's favorite team clearly has no bounds, a local hair salon even offered free blue mohawks to any brave volunteer willing to uniquely celebrate the Mavericks first trip to The NBA Finals in the team's 26-year history.

The enthusiasm inside the American Airlines Center reached a fever pitch as the sold-out crowd of more than 20,000 proudly waved white pompoms with flashing blue lights during the pre-game introductions. The Mavericks and their loyal devotees were fired up, as were the Miami Heat, a team also

making its first trip to The Finals. The matchup marked the first time since 1971 — when the Milwaukee Bucks defeated the Baltimore Bullets — that two teams were making their first appearances in the championship series.

The Finals would culminate in what many writers, broadcasters and fans were

saying were some of the most competitive strings of playoff series in recent years. Dramatic finishes resulting in a record nine games being decided in overtime, along with a record 14 games being determined by two points or fewer, certainly supported such claims. And, Game 1 of The NBA Finals didn't disappoint, following the same tension-filled pattern that was on nightly display since the playoffs tipped off in late April.

While first Finals game jitters can bring even some of the game's elite players to their knees, that certainly didn't apply to

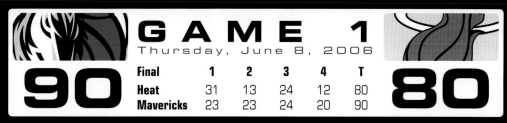

GAME 1
Thursday, June 8, 2006

	Final	1	2	3	4	T	
90	**Heat**	31	13	24	12	80	**80**
	Mavericks	23	23	24	20	90	

Dwyane Wade and the Heat as he hit six of his first seven shots for 13 points, easily slicing through Dallas' defense as Miami shot 70 percent for the period, leading 31-23.

The same couldn't be said for the Mavericks' Dirk Nowitzki and Josh Howard, who combined for two for 11 from the field in the quarter. Yet similar to what was witnessed routinely throughout these playoffs was the emergence of the role player and on this historic night, the best player on the floor wasn't named O'Neal, Wade or Nowitzki — he went by the nickname of "Jet." Jason Terry not only kept the Mavericks in the game, but propelled them one step closer to their championship dreams, hitting nine of his first 11 shots en route to 20 first-half points.

The Mavericks, who trailed by 11 at one point, closed out the quarter on a 12-3 run, punctuated by Nowitzki's jumper at the buzzer for a 46-44 lead. Terry was everywhere, penetrating, hitting runners, jumpers, even throwing down a dunk while his teammates struggled, shooting eight for 30 in the half.

The third quarter saw the Mavericks uncharacteristically turn the ball over seven times, a surprisingly high number considering they averaged only 10 per game during the regular season as they trailed 70-68 heading into the fourth.

But Terry, who didn't have a field goal attempt in the third quarter, wouldn't allow the Mavericks to lose their first Finals game. He reasserted himself on offense, hit four of six shots, including back-to-back three-pointers, en route to 12 fourth-quarter points.

"Jet" swooped in on defense as well, grabbing two key steals to keep Miami at bay, 82-79, as Dallas' defense limited the Heat to 12 points in the fourth, tying the second-fewest fourth-quarter points allowed in a Finals game in the shot-clock era.

Terry thrived in his first Finals appearance, shooting 13 for 18 (72 percent) from the floor, which was the fourth-highest field-goal percentage in a player's first Finals appearance. It was a much-needed game for the seven-year veteran, who failed to shoot 50 percent or score 20 points in any of the six Western Conference Finals games versus the Phoenix Suns.

"Jason Terry makes us a special team," Mavericks coach Avery Johnson said. "On a night like this with [Josh Howard and Dirk Nowitzki combining to hit seven of 28 shots], we need to get offense somewhere.

"We've been asking the real J.T. to come back to us," Johnson said. "We saw the real Jason Terry."

DALLAS Box Score

Starters	POS	MIN	FGM-A	3PM-A	FTM-A	OFF	DEF	TOT	AST	PF	ST	TO	BS	PTS
			Field Goals			**Rebounds**								
Adrian Griffin	G	13:18	4-6	0-0	0-0	1	0	1	1	1	1	0	0	8
Jason Terry	G	37:13	13-18	4-7	2-2	0	4	4	1	2	3	1	0	32
Dirk Nowitzki	F	39:11	4-14	2-4	6-6	2	8	10	4	2	3	2	0	16
Josh Howard	F	43:42	3-14	0-4	4-6	0	12	12	4	4	1	5	0	10
DeSagana Diop	C	16:25	0-0	0-0	0-0	1	1	2	0	2	1	2	2	0
Bench														
Jerry Stackhouse		29:00	4-11	0-2	5-6	0	5	5	4	1	0	3	1	13
Erick Dampier		27:01	3-4	0-0	2-4	3	4	7	0	4	0	0	0	8
Devin Harris		17:58	0-3	0-1	1-2	0	0	0	2	1	0	1	0	1
Keith Van Horn		10:53	1-2	0-0	0-0	0	2	2	0	0	0	0	0	2
Marquis Daniels		05:19	0-0	0-0	0-0	0	0	0	2	1	0	0	0	0
Josh Powell		DNP												
Darrell Armstrong		DNP												
TOTAL		240	32-72	6-18	20-26	7	36	43	18	18	9	14	3	90
			44.4%	33.3%	76.9%	Team Rebounds: 4						Total TO: 14		

MIAMI BoxScore

Starters	POS	MIN	Field Goals			Rebounds			AST	PF	ST	TO	BS	PTS
			FGM-A	3PM-A	FTM-A	OFF	DEF	TOT						
Jason Williams	G	34:12	5-11	2-5	0-0	0	4	4	4	3	1	1	0	12
Dwyane Wade	G	43:02	11-25	0-2	6-10	3	3	6	6	4	4	5	1	28
Udonis Haslem	F	33:14	2-4	0-0	0-0	3	6	9	0	5	0	1	0	4
Antoine Walker	F	42:15	7-19	3-9	0-0	0	6	6	4	3	1	6	0	17
Shaquille O'Neal	C	38:15	8-11	0-0	1-9	3	4	7	5	4	0	2	0	17
Bench														
James Posey		24:56	1-3	0-1	0-0	1	6	7	0	5	1	0	0	2
Gary Payton		18:46	0-4	0-3	0-0	2	3	5	1	1	3	0	0	0
Alonzo Mourning		5:20	0-1	0-0	0-0	0	1	1	0	1	0	0	0	0
Derek Anderson		DNP												
Jason Kapono		DNP												
Michael Doleac		DNP												
Shandon Anderson		DNP												
TOTAL		240	34-78	5-20	7-19	12	33	45	20	25	10	15	1	80
			43.6%	25.0%	36.8%	Team Rebounds: 10					Total TO: 16				

Stacked Deck

Mavs' Sixth Man Fuels Game 2 Win

The mood the day after the Heat's Game 1 loss was less than ideal. "I think our players are absolutely disgusted and they should be disgusted, disgusted and frustrated," Heat coach Pat Riley said. "[It] has nothing to do with anger." ❧ Heat center Alonzo Mourning described his team's overall effort. "Horrendous," he said.

At halftime of Game 2, the mood of the team would reach a new low, courtesy of a player who single handedly set the Heat adrift with a scoring barrage that helped change the complexion of not only the game, but the series as well.

With 1:20 remaining in the second quarter, the Heat were within six points, 40-34, despite withstanding a 13-0 Mavericks' run. Then, a flurry of Jerry Stackhouse three-pointers left them stunned.

With 1:19 remaining, Stackhouse drilled a baseline three-pointer, putting Dallas ahead, 43-34. Thirty-six seconds later, Stackhouse did it again, this time

converting a straightaway three-pointer as Dwyane Wade fouled him resulting in a four-point play to make it 47-34. With two seconds remaining in the half, Stackhouse punctuated his spectacular performance with a fall-away three-pointer from deep in the corner, capping the three-point clinic.

The frenetic finish whipped the capacity crowd of 20,459 at American Airlines Center into a frenzy as fans celebrated the Mavericks' 27-9 run. The score stood at 50-34 heading into the halftime locker room.

What seemed to be a close game was suddenly out of reach for the Heat, who never recovered in the second half as Dallas dictated the tempo. The Mavericks outworked Miami and forced a running game, while the defense foiled Shaquille O'Neal at every turn. Relentless pressure in the form of double

GAME 2						
Sunday, June 11, 2006						
99	Final	1	2	3	4	T	**85**
	Heat	17	17	24	27	**85**	
	Mavericks	18	32	32	17	**99**	

coverage relegated O'Neal to the bench for the entire fourth quarter along with a game total five field-goal attempts and a career-playoff-low five points.

Dirk Nowitzki bounced back from a subpar Game 1 performance with 26 points and 16 rebounds, complemented by Josh Howard's 15 points in 29 minutes.

However, the night belonged to the ultimate playoff sixth man who came within two points of outscoring the entire Heat bench. It's a practice to which Stackhouse is accustomed, having outscored the opposing bench nine previous times in the 2006 playoffs.

"You saw it years ago with the Detroit Pistons with Vinnie Johnson," said Mavericks head coach Avery Johnson. "To have that guy who can come off the bench and score is great — without even getting screens."

At one time, Stackhouse, who finished with 19 points and a season-high four three-pointers, was once one of the NBA's most prolific scorers, leading the league in total points when he averaged a career high 29.8 with the Detroit Pistons in the 2000-01 season. The third overall pick in the 1995 NBA Draft with the Philadelphia 76ers, Stackhouse passed the 14,000 point plateau this past season, his 11th in the NBA. Despite averaging a career low 13 points per game, it's the championship opportunity and not the individual accolades that drives Stackhouse.

"Everything I've gone through has helped me to be in this role now," Stackhouse said. "It's been a great ride. I've been with a team that won 18 games my rookie year, and, now, I'm on a team playing in The Finals."

That team, the Dallas Mavericks, now stood two victories away from Stackhouse's first championship.

DALLAS Box Score

Starters	POS	MIN	FGM-A	3PM-A	FTM-A	OFF	DEF	TOT	AST	PF	ST	TO	BS	PTS
Adrian Griffin	G	18:16	0-0	0-0	0-0	1	3	4	0	4	0	1	0	0
Jason Terry	G	41:17	6-15	1-6	3-5	0	1	1	9	2	2	3	0	16
Dirk Nowitzki	F	41:03	8-16	0-2	10-11	1	15	16	4	2	0	1	2	26
Josh Howard	F	28:33	6-12	2-3	1-1	1	2	3	1	5	0	4	2	15
DeSagana Diop	C	12:17	0-0	0-0	1-2	1	3	4	0	5	1	1	0	1
Bench														
Jerry Stackhouse		30:07	6-11	4-5	3-3	1	2	3	3	1	0	3	0	19
Erick Dampier		28:49	2-3	0-0	2-3	4	9	13	1	2	1	2	1	6
Devin Harris		23:11	4-10	0-1	3-3	0	1	1	4	4	1	1	0	11
Keith Van Horn		10:18	2-3	1-2	0-0	0	0	0	0	1	0	1	0	5
Marquis Daniels		6:09	0-0	0-0	0-0	0	1	1	1	1	0	1	0	0
Josh Powell	DNP													
Darrell Armstrong	DNP													
TOTAL		240	34-70	8-19	23-28	9	37	46	23	27	5	18	5	99
			48.6%	42.1%	82.1%	Team Rebounds: 4						Total TO: 19		

MIAMI BoxScore

Starters	POS	MIN	FGM-A	3PM-A	FTM-A	OFF	DEF	TOT	AST	PF	ST	TO	BS	PTS
Jason Williams	G	30:59	3-10	1-4	4-5	0	2	2	4	2	1	0	0	11
Dwyane Wade	G	40:00	6-19	0-0	11-14	4	4	8	3	4	2	4	1	23
Udonis Haslem	F	20:07	3-6	0-0	0-0	0	1	1	0	2	0	2	0	6
Antoine Walker	F	42:54	8-16	4-7	0-0	0	4	4	2	3	0	2	1	20
Shaquille O'Neal	C	27:56	2-5	0-0	1-7	1	5	6	2	1	0	2	0	5
Bench														
Gary Payton		27:59	1-4	0-2	0-0	0	1	1	4	2	2	0	0	2
James Posey		28:27	2-6	2-4	1-1	2	3	5	1	6	0	1	0	7
Alonzo Mourning		20:04	4-4	0-0	3-5	1	3	4	0	3	0	1	1	11
Shandon Anderson		1:34	0-0	0-0	0-0	0	1	1	0	0	0	1	0	0
Derek Anderson		DNP												
Jason Kapono		DNP												
Michael Doleac		DNP												
TOTAL		240	29-70	7-17	20-32	8	24	32	16	23	5	13	3	85
			41.4%	41.2%	62.5%	Team Rebounds: 12						Total TO: 13		

06 NBA FINALS
GAME 2 — June 11, 2006
Dallas Mavericks 99
Miami Heat 85

The Finals

MIAMI

HEAT

Wade a Comeback!

Heat Star Takes Over to Avert Finals Disaster

An air of excitement trumped any feelings of desperation as fans filed into AmericanAirlines Arena on yet another spectacular Miami evening. Despite being down 0-2, the Miami Heat faithful were jubilant over attending their first NBA Finals game in franchise history. No one was dwelling on the prospect that falling 0-3 in the Finals is a virtual death knell since no team has ever overcome such a deficit to win the championship.

After all, the hope and optimism was understandable. The Heat were at home, a place they had lost only once in the postseason, recording an 8-1 record heading into Game 3. After two quarters of play, the faithful were rewarded as Miami led 52-43, although the positive thoughts quickly faded in the third quarter. The Mavs went into full-throttle mode, pushing the tempo, exploding for 34 points while outscoring the Heat by 18. The outlook then went from bad to worse after Dwyane Wade picked up his fifth foul with 10:56 to play.

Trailing by 13 with 6:34 remaining and the crowd growing increasingly frustrated, Wade single handedly

GAME 3
Tuesday, June 13, 2006

98   **96**

Final	1	2	3	4	T
Mavericks	21	22	34	19	96
Heat	29	23	16	30	98

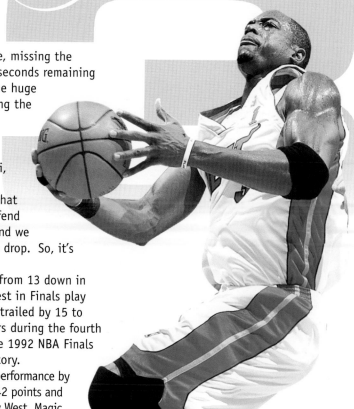

resuscitated a season lying in the balance as he willed the Heat back into the game, igniting a breathtaking 12-2 run. Wade was unstoppable despite a sore left knee — bank shot, jump shot, slashes to the basket — scoring nine points during the stretch.

"I kept looking up at the score thinking, 'I ain't going out like this,'" Wade said. "Not 3-0 [in games]. So, you do what you can."

What Wade did was *everything* as the sellout crowd sprung to life, tasting victory as the Heat suddenly surged ahead, 95-93, thanks, in large part, to clutch free-throw shooting by Shaquille O'Neal and Udonis Haslem.

While the Heat was white hot down the stretch, the Mavs were ice cold, going scoreless for nearly five minutes until Devin Harris tied the game with a driving layup with 33.5 seconds left. Miami surged ahead as Gary Payton picked the most opportune time to drain his only field goal of the game, a 16-foot jumper from the right side at the 9.3-second mark. Despite the breakdown, the Mavs had an opportunity to send the game into overtime after Dirk Nowitzki was fouled. Nowitzki, who entered the game shooting 94 percent from the free-throw line for the series, made his first attempt

and did the unthinkable, missing the second one with three seconds remaining as Wade pulled down the huge rebound, virtually sealing the Mavericks' fate.

"Maybe we started to relax too early or celebrate," said Nowitzki, who ended up with 30 points. "I don't know what it was, but we didn't defend them the way we had, and we couldn't get anything to drop. So, it's obviously frustrating."

The Heat's comeback from 13 down in the fourth was the largest in Finals play since the Chicago Bulls trailed by 15 to the Portland Trail Blazers during the fourth quarter of Game 6 in the 1992 NBA Finals en route to a 97-93 victory.

It was an exhilarating performance by Wade, who finished with 42 points and 13 rebounds, joining Jerry West, Magic Johnson and Michael Jordan as the only guards in Finals history to achieve a double-double in points and rebounds. A performance worthy of inclusion along with the many other magical Finals moments featured in ABC's Legacy of Champions opener.

"The basketball gods were good to us tonight," said Miami coach Pat Riley.

DALLAS Box Score

Starters	POS	MIN	FGM-A	3PM-A	FTM-A	OFF	DEF	TOT	AST	PF	ST	TO	BS	PTS
			Field Goals			Rebounds								
Adrian Griffin	G	14:16	1-3	0-0	0-0	1	4	5	3	3	2	1	0	2
Jason Terry	G	35:33	7-14	1-3	1-2	0	1	1	5	2	2	2	0	16
Dirk Nowitzki	F	44:44	9-20	2-7	10-12	0	7	7	1	5	0	3	0	30
Josh Howard	F	42:22	8-13	3-3	2-2	0	5	5	1	4	0	1	1	21
DeSagana Diop	C	10:54	0-0	0-0	0-0	1	3	4	0	4	0	0	0	0
Bench														
Jerry Stackhouse		31:26	1-9	0-1	2-2	0	1	1	1	2	1	2	0	4
Erick Dampier		29:24	6-7	0-0	2-5	5	4	9	0	4	3	1	1	14
Devin Harris		18:20	4-7	0-0	1-3	0	0	0	4	3	1	2	0	9
Keith Van Horn		8:32	0-2	0-2	0-0	0	2	2	0	2	0	2	0	0
Marquis Daniels		4:29	0-0	0-0	0-0	0	0	0	0	0	0	1	0	0
Darrell Armstrong		DNP												
Josh Powell		DNP												
TOTAL		240	36-75	6-16	18-26	7	27	34	15	29	9	15	2	96
			48.0%	37.5%	69.2%	Team Rebounds: 4						Total TO: 16		

MIAMI BoxScore

Starters	POS	MIN	FGM-A	3PM-A	FTM-A	OFF	DEF	TOT	AST	PF	ST	TO	BS	PTS
			Field Goals			**Rebounds**								
Dwyane Wade	G	43:05	14-26	1-2	13-18	2	11	13	2	5	2	1	0	42
Jason Williams	G	34:49	5-11	2-5	0-0	0	1	1	3	3	0	3	0	12
Udonis Haslem	F	34:13	3-8	0-0	2-6	8	3	11	0	4	3	3	0	8
Antoine Walker	F	35:23	6-17	0-5	0-2	1	6	7	1	3	0	2	0	12
Shaquille O'Neal	C	37:06	6-9	0-0	4-6	3	8	11	5	3	1	7	2	16
Bench														
James Posey		27:40	1-2	1-2	1-2	0	3	3	0	1	0	1	0	4
Gary Payton		19:09	1-1	0-0	0-0	1	1	2	2	1	1	2	0	2
Alonzo Mourning		8:35	1-2	0-0	0-0	1	0	1	0	3	2	1	0	2
Shandon Anderson		DNP												
Derek Anderson		DNP												
Michael Doleac		DNP												
Jason Kapono		DNP												
TOTAL		**240**	**37-76**	**4-14**	**20-34**	**16**	**33**	**49**	**13**	**23**	**9**	**20**	**2**	**98**
			48.7%	28.6%	58.8%	**Team Rebounds: 13**						**Total TO: 20**		

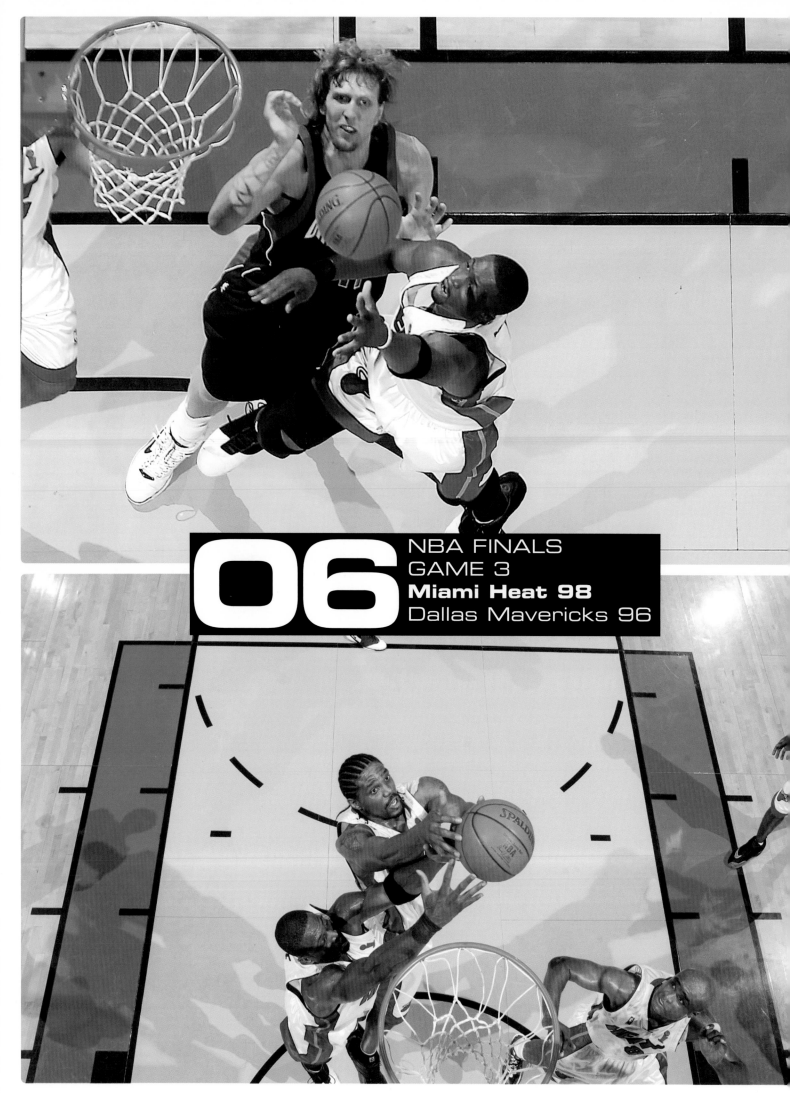

06 NBA FINALS
GAME 3
Miami Heat 98
Dallas Mavericks 96

The Finals

4

The Finals

No Stopping Wade
Heat Gain Control in Rout

How would the Mavericks respond after the 13-point, 6:34 meltdown of Game 3? Would Dallas be able to shake off the improbable loss and re-seize control of the series, or would the lingering effects be so great, so demoralizing that Miami already had the mental edge despite trailing by one game?

Those burning questions were not only emphatically answered, but a batch of troubling new ones arose for the Mavericks as the Heat regained control and momentum of the series only 48 minutes later.

Any hopes of the Mavericks re-establishing the series back in their favor began with adhering to its No. 1 defensive priority: contain Game 3 hero Dwyane Wade. Not a chance. Not on this night. Despite rotating three different defenders — Devin Harris, Josh Howard and Adrian Griffin — the Mavs were unsuccessful as Wade scored at will, eluding Maverick defenders as he dropped in 14 of the Heat's first 19 points in the first quarter.

When Shaquille O'Neal was sent to the bench with early foul trouble, the Heat received a boost from Alonzo Mourning, who set the defensive tone early with two first-quarter blocks.

Wade continued to have his way, scoring 24 points in the first half as the Mavs trailed by 10, 54-44, while only shooting 34 percent as Dirk Nowitzki and Josh Howard struggled, combining for 3 of 16 from the field.

The shooting woes would continue for the Mavericks in the second half, as they were unable to capitalize on the multitude of opportunities the Heat presented them. The Heat turned the ball over 13 times in a span of 13 minutes stemming from the seven-minute mark in

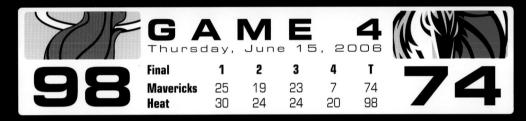

GAME 4 Thursday, June 15, 2006						
98	Final	1	2	3	4	T	**74**
	Mavericks	25	19	23	7	74	
	Heat	30	24	24	20	98	

the fourth, yet the Mavericks couldn't take advantage, unable to crack the 10-point deficit. After O'Neal converted two free throws as a result of a Jerry Stackhouse flagrant foul at the 6:29 mark, the Heat's lead grew to 18, and the realization that this series was undergoing a dramatic shift was taking shape.

Although the Mavs closed the gap to 11, 78-67, thanks to an 8-0 run entering the fourth quarter, poor shooting continued to plague Dallas. Its fate was sealed, missing 10 straight baskets during one stretch in the fourth quarter on its way to establishing a new Finals record for fewest points in a quarter with seven.

While Wade dazzled in another sensational outing with 36 points, the other story line for Miami was the huge play of their bench, which outscored their Mavs' counterparts, 23-22. James Posey scored 15 points and grabbed 10 rebounds and played big as starter Udonis Haslem picked up three early fouls. Mourning contributed four rebounds, three blocks and four points in nearly 14 minutes of spirited play.

"The bench was big," said Miami head coach Pat Riley who played 11 of his 12 players, including Shandon Anderson. "They're not a supporting cast. I don't look at it that way. They're all pros.

They've been around. They know what to do."

It was a forgettable evening for the Mavericks, who shot 31 percent from the field, lowlighted by Nowitzki and Howard, who combined for 3 of 22 shooting (.136). The Heat defense continued to successfully play up and in on Nowitzki, whose two-game shooting total in Miami now stood at 11 for 34 (.323).

"Now," Nowitzki said after the game, "Miami is playing with a lot of confidence."

MIAMI BoxScore

Starters	POS	MIN	FGM-A	3PM-A	FTM-A	OFF	DEF	TOT	AST	PF	ST	TO	BS	PTS
			Field Goals			**Rebounds**								
Dwyane Wade	G	39:38	13-23	2-5	8-9	0	6	6	3	4	1	4	1	36
Jason Williams	G	31:18	1-5	1-3	3-5	0	2	2	6	0	1	1	0	6
Udonis Haslem	F	17:56	1-2	0-0	0-0	0	2	2	1	5	2	4	0	2
Antoine Walker	F	39:12	5-11	2-6	2-2	0	3	3	2	2	2	0	1	14
Shaquille O'Neal	C	29:59	6-8	0-0	5-10	3	10	13	3	4	0	3	2	17
Bench														
James Posey		26:22	5-9	2-4	3-4	1	9	10	1	3	1	1	0	15
Gary Payton		19:35	1-2	0-0	0-2	0	1	1	4	0	2	0	2	2
Shandon Anderson		19:25	1-4	0-1	0-2	1	4	5	2	1	0	2	0	2
Alonzo Mourning		13:54	1-2	0-0	2-2	1	5	6	0	3	0	1	3	4
Jason Kapono		1:32	0-0	0-0	0-0	0	0	0	0	0	0	0	0	0
Michael Doleac		1:09	0-0	0-0	0-0	0	0	0	0	0	0	0	0	0
Derek Anderson	DNP													
TOTAL		240	34-66	7-19	23-36	6	42	48	19	26	7	18	7	98
			51.5%	36.8%	63.9%	Team Rebounds: 13					Total TO: 18			

DALLAS Box Score

Starters	POS	MIN	FGM-A	3PM-A	FTM-A	OFF	DEF	TOT	AST	PF	ST	TO	BS	PTS
Devin Harris	G	27:34	4-8	0-0	3-3	0	0	0	2	3	0	3	0	11
Jason Terry	G	32:52	8-18	1-5	0-1	0	1	1	0	2	1	3	0	17
Dirk Nowitzki	F	41:07	2-14	1-5	11-13	1	8	9	1	2	1	4	0	16
Josh Howard	F	35:45	1-8	0-4	1-2	1	6	7	2	4	2	1	0	3
DeSagana Diop	C	17:42	1-1	0-0	3-5	1	1	2	0	3	0	0	1	5
Bench														
Jerry Stackhouse		30:00	6-18	1-5	3-3	3	1	4	4	1	1	0	1	16
Erick Dampier		18:25	0-1	0-0	0-0	1	3	4	1	5	1	1	1	0
Adrian Griffin		16:48	3-3	0-0	0-0	3	3	6	0	2	0	0	0	6
Darrell Armstrong		6:15	0-2	0-1	0-0	0	1	1	0	0	0	0	0	0
Keith Van Horn		4:57	0-3	0-1	0-0	0	1	1	0	0	0	0	0	0
Marquis Daniels		4:57	0-2	0-1	0-0	0	0	0	0	0	0	1	0	0
Josh Powell		3:38	0-1	0-0	0-0	1	0	1	0	2	0	0	0	0
TOTAL		**240**	**25-79**	**3-22**	**21-27**	**11**	**25**	**36**	**10**	**24**	**6**	**13**	**3**	**74**
			31.6%	13.6%	77.8%		Team Rebounds: 8					Total TO: 14		

The Finals

The Finals

Instant Classic
Heat Take Command in OT Thriller

t was a fitting tribute, one that coincided perfectly with the NBA's celebration of its 60th postseason, highlighted by the greatest playoff moments in league history. A game worthy of immediate inclusion, bursting with all of the necessary hair-raising moments deemed necessary for timeless excellence status — clutch baskets, breathtaking plays, nonstop lead changes and virtuoso late-game heroics.

The fourth quarter and overtime session of Game 5 featured all of that and more as the Mavericks were determined to erase the seemingly indelible memories of its two previous unsuccessful performances in Miami. Boasting a 9-point lead in the third quarter, the momentum of the series appeared to be shifting in the Mavs' favor until a pair of Dwyane Wade baskets and a timely James Posey three-pointer punctuated a 7-0 Miami run as the third quarter drew to a close, setting the stage for the fourth-quarter dramatics.

"We got it down to 71-70 [to start the fourth quarter] and from there it was probably one of the greatest games I've ever been a part of. Everybody made big shots," said Miami Heat coach Pat Riley, who has witnessed a plethora of great games and moments in his 31 years in the NBA as a player and coach.

The parade of clutch baskets began when Dirk Nowitzki hit a 14-foot turnaround jumper with 49 seconds remaining to tie the game at 91. Nowitzki was at it again 29 seconds later, driving

GAME 5

Sunday, June 18, 2006

101

Final	1	2	3	4	OT	T
Mavericks	21	30	20	22	7	100
Heat	24	19	27	23	8	101

100

across the lane while eluding a crowd of defenders as he spotted a wide-open Erick Dampier near the basket for an easy dunk to give the Mavs a 93-91 lead.

Greatness is born out of pressure moments and Wade, who had

combined for 79 points in Games 3 and 4, routinely flourished when presented with such opportunities in this series. Wade, who had scored the last nine points for Miami, made it 11 after pulling up to the right side of the basket and kissing a short bank shot to tie the game with 2.8 seconds remaining. It was his 17th point of the quarter.

MIAMI BoxScore

	POS	MIN	FGM-A	3PM-A	FTM-A	OFF	DEF	TOT	AST	PF	ST	TO	BS	PTS
			Field Goals			**Rebounds**								
Dwyane Wade	G	50:06	11-28	0-2	21-25	0	4	4	4	1	3	3	0	43
Jason Williams	G	26:01	3-6	3-5	0-1	0	1	1	4	1	0	1	0	9
Udonis Haslem	F	29:26	1-3	0-0	0-0	2	2	4	0	6	0	1	0	2
Antoine Walker	F	26:09	2-7	1-4	1-2	0	2	2	2	4	0	2	0	6
Shaquille O'Neal	C	47:22	8-12	0-0	2-12	2	10	12	1	5	2	3	0	18
Bench														
James Posey		44:19	2-6	2-5	4-4	2	4	6	0	5	2	1	0	10
Gary Payton		30:09	3-5	1-1	1-1	0	2	2	2	4	0	0	0	8
Shandon Anderson		07:16	1-2	0-0	2-2	1	0	1	1	0	0	0	0	4
Alonzo Mourning		04:11	0-0	0-0	1-2	0	1	1	0	0	0	0	0	1
Derek Anderson		DNP	-	-	-									
Jason Kapono		DNP	-	-	-									
Michael Doleac		DNP	-	-	-									
TOTAL		**265**	**31-69**	**7-17**	**32-49**	**7**	**26**	**33**	**14**	**26**	**7**	**11**	**0**	**101**
			44.9%	41.2%	65.3%	Team Rebounds: 16					Total TO: 12			

The spellbinding play for both teams continued in the overtime session when Gary Payton sliced through the Mavericks' defense to hit a driving, high-arching layup off the glass to give the Heat a one-point lead. Nowitzki responded on the next possession, delivering a baseline fadeaway over the outstretched fingertips of a hard-charging Shaquille O'Neal — Mavs 100, Heat 99 — with nine seconds remaining.

The Heat called time out. Dwyane Wade wanted the ball, demanded the ball. It didn't matter that he shot only 10 for 27 from the field, Wade had carried the Heat on his back since the series shifted to Miami, and he wasn't about to let up. Not now, not with so much at stake.

Inbounding the ball at halfcourt, Wade caught a pass all the way in the backcourt and immediately made his move. Driving with a single-minded determination, Wade dribbled on the right side of the court as three Mavs' defenders collapsed on him. Regardless, he somehow managed to slice his way to the hoop as he was fouled with one second remaining.

Clearly immune to any Finals pressure, Wade calmly sank the first free throw to

tie the game at 100 as the 20,145 fans at sold-out America Airlines Arena recognized the Finals history unfolding before their eyes. When Josh Howard called timeout after the basket, confusion ensued as the Mavericks' bench pleaded to the officials that the break in the action was intended after the second free throw. The timeout stood as replays showed Howard clearly signaled for the break, not once, but twice. Wade calmly sank the second free throw to give the Heat a 101-100 lead as Devin Harris' desperation heave fell short at the buzzer.

The legend of Dwyane Wade had taken root as another spectacular Finals chapter was completed, while the final buzzer confirmed yet another frustrating night for the Mavericks, who were minus a suspension-serving Jerry Stackhouse for his excessively hard foul on O'Neal.

"We took care of business at home like we're supposed to," said Wade, who established a new Finals record for made free throws with 21, surpassing Bob Pettit's 1958 record of 19. "We won three games, two in dramatic fashion. Now we've got to win one on the road."

DALLAS Box Score

Starters	POS	MIN	FGM-A	3PM-A	FTM-A	OFF	DEF	TOT	AST	PF	ST	TO	BS	PTS
			Field Goals			**Rebounds**								
Devin Harris	G	33:58	2-12	0-1	2-2	0	1	1	1	5	1	0	0	6
Jason Terry	G	50:17	13-23	4-9	5-5	1	4	5	1	2	1	4	0	35
Dirk Nowitzki	F	49:02	8-19	0-4	4-5	2	6	8	3	4	0	2	0	20
Josh Howard	F	50:03	8-17	0-3	9-11	5	5	10	3	4	0	3	0	25
DeSagana Diop	C	20:47	1-2	0-0	0-0	1	3	4	0	6	0	0	0	2
Bench														
Erick Dampier		19:20	2-2	0-0	1-2	0	8	8	0	5	0	2	0	5
Adrian Griffin		15:21	1-2	0-0	0-0	1	1	2	1	3	1	1	0	2
Marquis Daniels		13:58	2-3	1-1	0-0	0	0	0	4	3	0	1	0	5
Didier Ilunga-Mbenga		08:02	0-0	0-0	0-0	0	3	3	0	4	0	1	0	0
Keith Van Horn		04:31	0-1	0-1	0-0	1	0	1	0	2	0	0	0	0
Jerry Stackhouse		DNP												
Darrell Armstrong		DNP												
TOTAL		**265**	**37-81**	**5-19**	**21-25**	**11**	**31**	**42**	**13**	**38**	**3**	**14**	**0**	**100**
			45.7%	26.3%	84.0%	Team Rebounds: 12					Total TO: 16			

NBA FINALS
GAME 5 – June 18, 2006
Miami Heat 101
Dallas Mavericks 100

06

The Finals

Championship Bliss
Confident Heat Capture Title

The championship tone was set by none other than the master motivator himself. "I packed one suit, one shirt and one tie," Miami head coach Pat Riley said prior to Game 6. "That's it." ☞ The supreme confidence was understandable. The Heat, by becoming only the second home team in NBA Finals history to sweep the middle three games, were firmly in control of the series. Yet, this was a

different Mavericks team at home, owners of the NBA's second best home record throughout the regular season. Since each team held serve thus far in the series, many expected the pattern to hold form, raising the likelihood of Game 7. Everyone, that is, except Riley and his players.

"He said, 'Leave the bags in the room, and they'll come get them,'" Shandon Anderson said in reference to Riley's directive that the team check out of their hotel before Game 6. "That set the tone right there."

After 10-plus minutes into the first quarter, it appeared the Heat would need to seek shelter from the storm as the Mavericks, feeding off its home crowd, surged to a 26-12 lead, thanks to the much maligned Dirk Nowitzki, who asserted himself at the outset, scoring 11 points off of a variety of shots.

The Heat withstood the Mavericks' charge, whittling away the lead courtesy of a smaller lineup. With Shaquille O'Neal sidelined, Dwyane Wade scored 13 points in a six-and-a-half minute stretch, while Alonzo Mourning provided plenty of lift off the bench, including an emphatic dunk in transition before halftime, capping off a 13-0 run as the Heat enjoyed its first lead of the game.

While the Mavericks settled for jump shots to open the third quarter, the Heat continued to attack, highlighted by Wade's block of a Nowitzki shot. Mourning was

a shot-blocking machine — denying consecutive attempts while throwing down a super-charged dunk on the other end as the Heat raced to a 68-59 lead.

The sold-out crowd at American Airlines Center grew anxious as the Heat appeared firmly in control of the game and, ultimately, its first championship until Marquis Daniels infused new life into the building. Daniels scored five straight points, broken up by two Nowitzki free throws and then followed that with another free throw, to narrow the gap 70-67, in favor of Miami. Back to back Josh Howard free throws tied the game at 79 with 7:06 remaining but that was the closest the Mavs would get. The Heat maintained the lead, thanks to timely baskets by Udonis Haslem and a huge three-pointer by James

Final	1	2	3	4	T
Heat	23	26	22	24	95
Mavericks	30	18	20	24	92

GAME 6
Tuesday, June 20, 2006

95   **92**

Posey with 3:43 remaining. The Mavs fought to the very end as Jason Terry's three-point attempt, which would have tied the game with two seconds remaining, barely missed.

It was a fitting close to a series packed with dramatic shifts throughout as the Heat joined the 1969 Boston Celtics and 1977 Portland Trail Blazers as the only teams in Finals history to win four straight games after losing the first two of the series. That is quite an accomplishment for a team that featured nine new players from the previous seasons and plenty more doubts among observers who questioned not only the mix, but,

whether the team had enough to win the championship.

"That's what makes it sweet, because not at one moment did one of us not believe in each other," said Wade, who earned NBA Finals MVP honors and plenty of Michael Jordan comparisons after averaging 34.7 points for the series. "No matter what, in the locker room, it was 15 strong."

That rallying cry — 15 Strong — was etched in more than 120,000 motivational cards, which featured photos of players and their wives, along with goals, reminding the players to stick together. The cards, which were kept under close wraps in the Heat's locker room, were finally sprung free and tossed around in a wild celebration.

"There was a lot of conjecture throughout the course of the year about our team, about the character, about certain players, [how] it wouldn't work, the chemistry," said Riley, who tasted his first champagne since leading the Los Angeles Lakers to a title in 1988. "People don't know how much these guys really wanted it."

MIAMI BoxScore

Starters	POS	MIN	FGM-A	3PM-A	FTM-A	OFF	DEF	TOT	AST	PF	ST	TO	BS	PTS
Jason Williams	G	45:24	10-18	0-0	16-21	3	7	10	5	4	4	5	3	36
Dwyane Wade	G	30:27	1-7	1-7	0-0	0	1	1	7	0	0	2	0	3
Udonis Haslem	F	40:30	8-13	0-0	1-4	4	6	10	1	3	2	3	0	17
Antoine Walker	F	33:30	6-17	0-6	2-3	3	8	11	2	2	1	0	1	14
Shaquille O'Neal	C	30:19	4-11	0-0	1-4	3	9	12	1	5	0	2	1	9
Bench														
James Posey		25:13	2-5	1-4	1-2	0	5	5	0	2	2	3	0	6
Gary Payton		17:51	1-3	0-1	0-0	0	1	1	2	3	0	2	0	2
Alonzo Mourning		14:03	3-4	0-0	2-3	1	5	6	0	4	0	1	5	8
Shandon Anderson		02:43	0-0	0-0	0-0	0	0	0	0	0	0	1	0	0
Derek Anderson	DNP													
Jason Kapono	DNP													
Michael Doleac	DNP													
TOTAL		240	35-78	2-18	23-37	14	42	56	18	23	9	19	10	95
			44.9%	11.1%	62.2%	Team Rebounds: 12						TOTAL TO: 19		

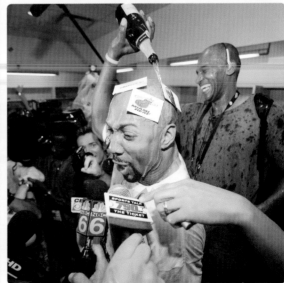

DALLAS Box Score

Starters	POS	MIN	FGM-A	3PM-A	FTM-A	OFF	DEF	TOT	AST	PF	ST	TO	BS	PTS
			Field Goals			**Rebounds**								
Devin Harris	G	25:53	2-4	0-0	2-3	3	0	3	4	5	2	4	0	6
Jason Terry	G	43:00	7-25	2-11	0-0	0	1	1	5	1	2	2	0	16
Dirk Nowitzki	F	47:02	10-22	1-2	8-8	3	12	15	2	5	0	1	2	29
Josh Howard	F	30:16	5-16	0-2	4-4	3	9	12	0	5	4	1	1	14
DeSagana Diop	C	16:05	1-3	0-0	0-1	0	4	4	1	3	0	0	2	2
Bench														
Jerry Stackhouse		29:17	5-13	2-6	0-0	1	3	4	3	5	2	3	1	12
Erick Dampier		24:52	0-1	0-0	1-2	3	5	8	0	2	1	2	1	1
Marquis Daniels		18:02	4-6	0-1	4-5	2	0	2	1	2	0	0	0	12
Adrian Griffin		04:20	0-2	0-0	0-0	1	0	1	0	0	1	0	0	0
Didier Ilunga-Mbenga		01:13	0-0	0-0	0-0	0	0	0	0	0	0	0	0	0
Keith Van Horn		DNP												
Darrell Armstrong		DNP												
TOTAL		240	34-92	5-22	19-23	16	34	50	16	28	12	13	7	92
			37.0%	22.7%	82.6%	TEAM REBS: 1				TOTAL TO: 13				

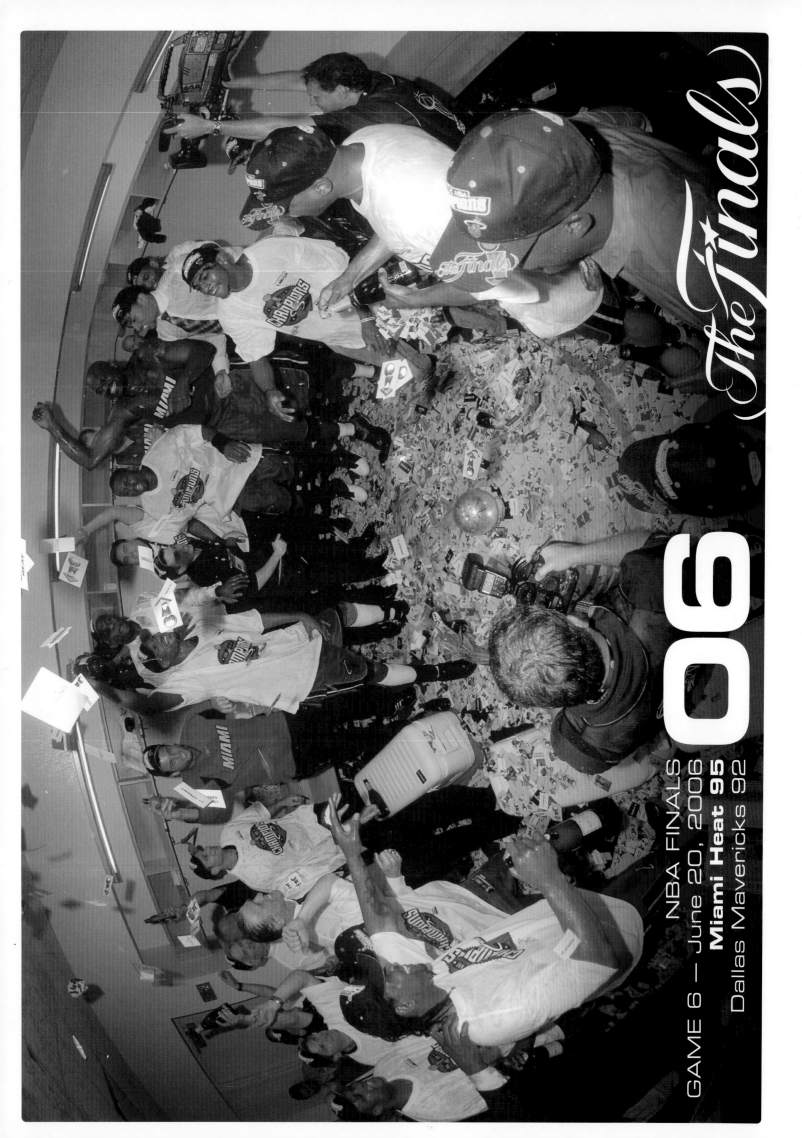

GAME 6 – June 20, 2006
NBA FINALS

06 06

Miami Heat 95
Dallas Mavericks 92

(The Finals)